Toward a North American Common Market

WITHDRAWN

Toward a North American Common Market

Problems and Prospects for a New Economic Community

EDITED BY

Charles F. Bonser

WITH CONTRIBUTIONS BY

Randall Baker & Joseph Miller
Lawrence R. Klein
Peter W. Ludlow
Gary C. Hufbauer & Jeffrey J. Schott

Westview Press
BOULDER • SAN FRANCISCO • OXFORD

Copyright © 1991 by Westview Press, Inc.

Published in 1991 in the United States of America by Westview Press, Inc., 5500 Central Avenue, Boulder, Colorado 80301, and in the United Kingdom by Westview Press, 36 Lonsdale Road, Summertown, Oxford OX2 7EW

Library of Congress Cataloging-in-Publication Data
Toward a North American common market : problems and prospects for a
   new economic community / edited by Charles F. Bonser.
      p.   cm.
   Includes bibliographical references.
   ISBN 0-8133-8127-4
   1. North America—Economic integration.   2. Europe—Economic
integration.   I. Bonser, Charles F.
HC95.T69   1991
337.1'7—dc20   91-11628
                                                                                    CIP

Printed and bound in the United States of America

The paper used in this publication meets the requirements
of the American National Standard for Permanence of Paper
for Printed Library Materials Z39.48-1984.

10   9   8   7   6   5   4   3   2   1

Contents

Tables and Figures

Preface

In February 1989 a small group of Indiana University international specialists were assembled by the University's Institute for Development Strategies to explore the idea of holding a high-level colloquium focused on the prospects for a North American Economic Community. The individuals participating in the session are listed below.

The group of I.U. experts agreed that such a program could make a valuable contribution to the "trialogue" on the subject and worked with the Institute for Development Strategies to select major presenters, participants, and to plan the event. The Colloquium was held at the Johnson Foundation's Wingspread Conference Center, April 26-28, 1990.

The subsequent announcement in June 1990 by Presidents Bush and Salinas that the United States and Mexico had agreed to initiate talks on a possible Free Trade Agreement verified our judgement about the importance of the issue.

This volume is based on the papers commissioned for the colloquium, and on the panel and open discussions that were conducted at Wingspread. I would like to thank the planning committee for their many contributions to what turned out to be a very successful and timely seminar. I would also like to thank the Ameritech Foundation, whose support of our Institute's program made this effort possible; the Canadian Government for their financial assistance to the colloquium; and the Johnson Foundation for making available their beautiful Wingspread Conference Center and providing logistical support and hospitality for the meetings.

Obviously, the success of any meeting of this kind is primarily dependent on the background, skill, and openness of the participants. The four papers we commissioned for the meetings were outstanding and more than provided the foundation we needed for our discussions. Our panel discussants were well-prepared, to the point, and were successful in raising the relevant issues pertinent to the topic. The group discussions were thoughtful, articulate, stimulating, and fun. I am particularly grateful to the colloquium participants for taking time from their busy schedules to be with us for this event and for the open and candid way in which they participated in what turned out to be almost two days of wall-to-wall debate.

Finally, I would be remiss if I did not extend special thanks to my Doctoral Assistant, Julie Bivin, who was indispensable in planning and implementing the Wingspread meeting, and to my Executive Secretary, Nancy Croker, who did yeoman work in all phases leading to the successful completion of the event and in seeing this volume to completion.

Charles F. Bonser
Director
Institute for Development Strategies
Indiana University

1

Introduction

Charles F. Bonser

The United States, Canada, and Mexico clearly have complementary strengths that could benefit from closer economic ties. The idea of moving toward economic integration between the three countries is, therefore, not new, and has been raised, from time to time, by various individuals or organizations. Indeed, President Reagan proposed a "North American Common Market" during his first campaign for the Presidency. President Bush, in his 1988 campaign, also promised to work toward a North American free trade zone. Thus, in spite of the fact that there are very real political and economic problems associated with expanding the US-Canadian Free Trade Agreement to include Mexico, it is not surprising that current events have made such a prospect more than theoretical.

The agreement between the United States and Canada to establish a Free Trade Area to be fully effective by 1998 offers a major pillar for a North American Economic Community. Mexico, under new political leadership, has retreated from its previous pattern of economic protectionism, and has been undertaking reforms that have substantially improved its economic climate and its ability to contribute to and profit from a freer trading framework. In June 1990 the Mexican Senate approved a move to seek an FTA with the United States. President Salinas commented at that time, "Mexico will not be left out of the new world configuration. The speed of the changes requires decisive answers on all fronts, in all markets."

Factors external to North America are obviously affecting the timeliness of such a possibility. These include:

1.   The European Community's efforts to finalize their own economic integration by 1992, and the uncertain nature of its future trade posture vis-á-vis non-European nations. The EC also has negotiations underway with the EFTA states (Austria, Finland, Norway, Sweden, Switzerland, Iceland) concerning future trade relations, and has undertaken preliminary discussions with several Eastern European countries about the future of their economic relations with the Community.

2.   Australia and New Zealand have an established Free Trade Area, and have initiated discussions for an Asia-Pacific "regional cooperation organization." The Association of Southeast Asian Nations (ASEAN) officials (Thailand, Indonesia, Malaysia, the Philippines, and Brunei) have expressed concern about the EC 1992 changes, and the Europeans' past record of erecting trade barriers such as market sharing, quotas, and local content requirements. At their July 1990 meeting in Jakarta there was much discussion about trade cooperation, and indications that ASEAN would open treaty negotiations.

3.   There has so far been a notable lack of accomplishment in the current Uruguay Round of Talks on the General Agreement on Trade and Tariffs (GATT). If the talks conclude in December 1990 without considerably more progress than has been indicated so far, it is likely that there will be more interest in the establishment of regional trading blocs in the world economy. As regrettable as some would view that development, the US, Canada, and Mexico would form a large, powerful market of its own—upwards of 355 million people—which would be more potent in negotiations with other blocs than any of the three would be alone.

All of these factors combined led those of us associated with the Institute for Development Strategies to conclude that the US, Canada, and Mexico should at least now carefully consider the principal issues, and the benefits and costs of closer economic integration. The four papers that were commissioned by the Institute for the Wingspread Colloquium are published here in the order in which they were presented. Together they provided a foundation for wide-ranging discussions about the desirability, likelihood, format, and problems of a move toward a North American Economic Community.

The paper by Randall Baker and Joseph Miller, "An Advocacy Case for a North American Economic Community," was meant to set the "data base" stage for the debate. Lawrence R. Klein's paper, "Global Markets in International Trade," focuses on the likely course of world trade into the next century, and the possibility of trading blocs developing. The paper by Peter Ludlow, "The European Community, EFTA, and the New Europe," provided to the Colloquium a European view of one of the most important external forces influencing the development of a North American Economic Community—the ascendancy of the EC, its likely future character, and its impact on the architecture of Europe and trading relationship implications with the rest of the world. Finally, the paper by Gary C. Hufbauer and Jeffrey Schott explores "The Realities of a North American Economic Alliance."

In the concluding chapter of this monograph I try to capture the essence of the discussions that took place at the colloquium. Key elements of the discussion are summarized, and main themes of the debate are categorized and presented. Finally, I draw conclusions—my own, not those of the colloquium—on where the issue seems to be heading, and what is the most desirable course of action for public policy in the region.

In order to provide an easy reference for the main themes of this monograph, the remainder of this Introductory chapter summarizes the primary points from the four papers that provided the basic source material for the discussion.

The Baker/Miller Advocacy Case

The Baker/Miller paper begins with a review of the economic relations between Canada and the US going back to about 1930. They make the point that, in spite of sometimes rocky political relations, and efforts by various Canadian governments over the years to pull closer to Europe, the share of Canadian exports to the United Kingdom dropped from 17.4% to about 3.8% between 1958 and 1978. During this same period, Canadian exports to the US grew from 55.9% to 70.3% of total exports. The importance of Canadian exports to the European Community dropped from 13.1% in 1980 to 6.5% in 1988. Today, Canada is the US's largest trading partner, receiving 21% of US exports. Canadian exports to the US constitute 75-80% of their total exports, and account for 20% of Canada's GNP.

The recognition by the Canadians of the importance of preserving this trading relationship, the movement of Britain into a continental Europe orbit, and the concern on the part of both Canada and the US that it was important to avoid trade disputes and protectionist measures that would disrupt trade, were major factors leading to the signing of the Free Trade Agreement on January 2, 1988.

Baker and Miller review the important provisions of the US-Canadian FTA, and report on some of the research on the economic impact of the agreement on several industries, and on the overall real output of the two countries. On balance, although there were some disappointments in the details of the FTA, they look for positive long-term results from the Agreement for both nations.

The authors also look to the history of the trade relationship between the US and Mexico. The primary pattern of industrial development in Mexico beginning about 1940 has been to "nurture and protect Mexican industry from foreign competition." In other words, their approach was to utilize import substitution, rather than an export-led model of development. The US approach to Mexico has varied from benign neglect to activist involvement through such programs as the World War II "Braceros" (worker importation) program, and later involvement in its replacement, the *"maquiladora"* program of tariff and trade concessions to manufacturers (initially) located on Mexico's northern border with the US.

The huge expansion of the Mexican oil industry, in concert with the OPEC oil embargoes of the 1970s, accelerated Mexican protectionism, and exacerbated its productivity problems. In 1982, with the oil industry in recession, Mexico announced it could not service its foreign debt. Drastic actions by the Mexican government followed. These included import restrictions, large cuts in public expenditures, and an 80% devaluation of the peso. Capital flowed out of the country, and unemployment soared. While progress was made in getting a runaway situation under control, in 1986 Mexico still "registered a 4% decline in growth, a 10.7% reduction in gross fixed investment, a 3.8% decline in manufacturing activity, and the loss of 1.5 million jobs."

Miller and Baker comment on how remarkable it is, given this situation as recently as four years ago, that the economic reforms introduced by the De La Madrid and Salinas governments have been able to turn the Mexican economy around. The inflation rate was cut from 224% at the end of 1987, to 15% at year-end in 1988. Mexico shifted from an import substitution model to an export-led model of development during this period. Its manufacturing exports grew 10% per year from 1986 through 1988. By the end of 1988, Mexico had replaced West Germany as the United States' third ranked trading partner, after Canada and Japan. The US accounted for 70% of its total exports.

Given this Mexican transformation, the authors direct their attention to the future. "How feasible is it to go much further with the present liberalization arrangements?" They conclude, in agreement with the Bilateral Commission, that, "Without a positive, shared vision of the future, bilateral economic relations will increasingly become occasions for conflict, instead of cooperation and growth. ... Furthermore, the high degree of connectivity in trade between Mexico and the US is unlikely to change significantly. . . .This sense of the inevitable may well have been a major factor in the ultimately successful passage of the Canadian Free Trade legislation. The establishment of a legislated framework of guaranteed access to the United States, at truly competitive terms, would provide Mexico with the climate of confidence necessary to keep its momentum going." As they later note in their paper, they would also "be locked into a system that would eliminate most of the threats of being closed out of a northern club."

Canada has much less trade and interaction with Mexico than does the United States. But Baker and Miller point out that the Canadian Senate Standing Committee on Foreign Affairs has expressed sympathy for an expansion of the Free Trade Area to include a "third party." However, in Baker and Miller's opinion, the problems of integrating Mexico "into a trade community would be potentially much more disruptive (than Canada), since the country's economy is more protected and more underdeveloped .... there would be a need for a realistic period of transition to allow Mexico to adjust." While not easy, they point out that the European Community has been able to handle equally difficult integration problems with less developed nations such as Portugal and Greece.

There have as yet been no detailed econometric studies that would offer estimates about the economic impact of an expanded Free Trade Area to include the Mexicans. (This is an important research need that the Institute for Development Strategies hopes to begin meeting in 1991.) The authors do provide analyses that support a favorable economic impact for both Mexico and the US based on improvements in efficiency and "industry dynamism."

In the final sections of their paper the authors ask, and answer the question, "What next?" They explore the steps necessary to the eventual establishment of an economic community; and they look at the foreign policy alternatives facing the United States in relation to a North American Economic Community. They see positive benefits for the United States in such a development, and basically no alternative for the Mexicans in their drive to obtain growth and stability. They also predict that the first step, a free trade agreement between the US and Mexico, will be reached "in the relatively near future." (It looks like the subsequent announcement by Presidents Bush and Salinas of the opening of negotiations for an FTA will result in their forecast being overtaken by events.) This must inevitably be followed by opening the flow of both capital and labor between the countries.

Lawrence Klein: Global Markets and Trading Blocs

Lawrence Klein's paper provides a detailed look at the way in which world trade patterns have evolved since the end of World War II. He suggests that with the development of more open multilateral trading relationships, "there was a flowering of economic performance that was clearly associated with the expansion of world trade." While there was a lessening of trade growth in the 1970s and early 1980s, he believes that some of the developments now underway in Europe, as well as other parts of the world, will lead to an expansion of global trade in the years ahead.

While obviously preferring a multilateral trading system, Klein sees "a world moving in the direction of the establishment of trading zones held together by bilateral agreements or by a strong institutional framework, as in the case of the European Community." Within this pattern, he expects the evolution of three principal trading groups in the years ahead: Europe—for now the EC and EFTA, but later Eastern Europe and perhaps even the Soviet Union; North America—where he sees the "real possibility of fashioning a North American Common Market"; and Asia-Pacific—where there is "an excellent fit among the economies of South East Asia and the Pacific."

His paper then provides current statistics on the flow on world trade in the key components of these regions, and later provides projections of world trade for the next five years. He sees a "world economy that gets reasonably soon to a 3% growth path for output, nurtured by a trade expansion that is between 5 and 6%, after a slowdown in 1990." He also believes this forecast could be conservative, given the developments in Eastern Europe and the end of the Cold War.

Peter Ludlow and the New Europe

For those readers who have been exposed to the range of opinion in the debate now underway about the future character and architecture of the European continent, Peter Ludlow's paper might best be described as a quintessential Europeanist view of the "new Europe." Given the fact that current developments in Europe will play a fundamental role (25% of world trade goes on in the EC and EFTA) in the nature of the global trading system into the next century, his analysis of the particulars of the evolution of the European Community—where it is heading, and its relationship to other European regions—provides important insights for the question of North American economic policy.

Ludlow makes a convincing argument that the European Community, essentially as now constituted, plus the European Free Trade Area (or as he puts it, the "EC-EFTA bloc," or, "The European Economic Space") are the relevant models for a North American Economic Community, rather the EC as such. He sees the EC of the future as being more directly comparable to the United States. In other words, a de facto "United States of Europe."

In the first section of his paper he walks us through the development of the EC, and discusses how the institutional structure of the Community came into its own. In his words:

> The European Community is about the promotion of greater wealth through the liberalization of trade and the development of other common policies. It is an economic community. It has always, however, been still more a political venture; a sustained effort, first to modify the natural inclinations and unruly behavior of member states which had led to several disastrous wars, and secondly to mould the same states into a new political entity, variously

defined in Community documents as a Federation or, more commonly, a Union.

Recent decisive steps taken toward this goal began in 1985 when Commission Secretary General, Jacques Delors, convinced "even the most reluctant Europeans" that if they really wanted a single market to be established, they would have to eliminate the veto system of governance that had prevailed until then in important Community matters. The result is known as the "qualified majority" voting system—essentially a weighted system of voting favoring the larger States. With that accomplished, "he initiated a process in which the inherent strengths of the institutions were unleashed in many areas of Community policy." These have included the 1992 goal of a "single market," and agreements to proceed toward Economic and Monetary Union.

In his exploration of the EC-EFTA relationship, Ludlow raises, and deals with, the question of whether a "Free Trade Area strategy is viable over time for the neighbors of a Union as large and powerful as the European Community." In 1984 a decision was taken by the EC and EFTA to "transform the largest system of trade in the world . . . into a dynamic European economic space." They agreed to work together on a number of fronts, the most important of which were trade policy questions such as standards, technical barriers, border facilities, rules of origin, unfair trade practices, state aids and access to government procurement. Particularly important in our context is that they also agreed to work together on such multilateral issues as the OECD, GATT, IMF, and the World Bank—in other words, to act as a bloc on world trading issues.

The period between 1985 and 1989 was less than conclusive in terms of whether this cooperative goal was going to be reached. Then Delors, in a speech in January 1989, proposed a new "two pillar" relationship in which EFTA would be a privileged partner of the EC, jointly responsible for the administration of the "European Economic Space." This led to negotiations in 1990, with a goal of completing the process by 1991.

Ludlow sees the outcome of these negotiations as resulting in the EFTA role becoming one of participating in Community decision "shaping," rather than as an equal partner in decision "making." The eventual form of the EC-EFTA relationship has implications beyond the two groups of nations. In light of the developments in Eastern Europe, the nature of the trading relationship will be an indicator of how the EC is likely to deal with the newly emerging democracies in the East. The nature of these relationships will eventually go beyond economic issues and include security matters as well.

Ludlow sees the emergence of an "EC hegemon" that will "create challenges for the global economy as a whole. It goes without saying that structural changes will have to be made in groups such as the G-7." He also believes we are heading toward a "world order based on trading blocs or zones." In his view, however, while there will be a need for skillful negotiation in order to achieve an orderly transition, this development "provides grounds for hope rather than despair."

Hufbauer and Schott on the Realities of the Proposition

The Hufbauer/Schott paper looks at the politics as well as the economics of a possible North American Common Market, and examines the benefits and costs to each of the three countries. While they argue that a "North American economic alliance cannot be the centerpiece of commercial diplomacy in any of the three nations," there are sufficient political and economic benefits to each, that "a coherent North American economic alliance seems an odds on favorite by the year 2000."

The balance of their paper then lays out possible paths and forms such an alliance might take. They define two alternative goals for an alliance: a "high goal," that they describe as a "North American Economic Community (NAEC)," and a "low goal" entitled a "North American Free Trade Area (NAFTA)." The political and economic "realities" of these alternatives are then detailed.

The Hufbauer/Schott "high road" goal is presented with two distinct paths "in which a grand leap is made over two to four years." The "low road is traveled step by step over a longer period." They conclude that the "high road" is not plausible, and that a better strategy would be to "sketch the goal in the broadest strokes, and then fill in the details step by step as political opportunity permits." They then lay out an "agenda" for a North American Free Trade Area that would make this proposed institutional change a reality. Finally, they caution against the proposed NAFTA becoming a discriminatory regional bloc that would erect barriers against outsiders, and damage the international economic system.

The Discussions

Each of the papers presented were followed by from two to four panelists reacting to the paper. These commentaries were recorded, along with the ensuing debate. The discussions of the group in attendance at the colloquium were wide-ranging and intense. Those participants who held official positions with one of the three governments necessarily made it clear that they were not speaking officially, or as representatives of their government. Rather, the discussion was held much as it would be in an academic setting. The group also decided that they would not, as a group, try to reach an agreement or conclusions about the policy issues under discussion. Thus, as noted above, any conclusions drawn from the sum of the various presentations and the colloquium debate are mine, and do not necessarily represent those of the group or any of the individuals participating in the Wingspread Colloquium.

2

Canada, the United States, and Mexico: An Advocacy Case for a North American Community

Randall Baker
Joseph Miller

Prologue

In this paper we have responded to a request to present the case for a North American Economic Community consisting of Canada, the United States, and Mexico. We wish to stress, at the outset, that ours is a position of *advocacy* rather than any attempt to be broadly "objective," "even-handed," or "unbiased." This advocacy paper will then form the basis for a discussion.

The paper examines the two cases individually because their cultural and economic bases are very different, and Canada has already entered into a Free Trade Agreement with the United States that will take full effect at the end of this decade. Mexico, on the other hand, has only begun negotiations in June 1990 with the United States on a free trade agreement. What these two countries, Canada and Mexico, have in common is not a link with each other, for the amount of mutual economic exchange is minimal, but a growing reorientation toward the United States in terms of their trade. In the case of Canada this began in the 1960s and has eroded the older links with Europe; in the case of Mexico it has replaced a long history of extremely protected production for the domestic market, import substitution, and a more typically third-world trade pattern with the United States.

Despite the growth of "border problems" in the relations between the United States and Mexico during the 1980s, despite an apparent growing concern about cultural domination among the Canadians, there appears to be strong evidence for an underlying tide of economic realism regarding closer trading links with the United States. In this paper we explore reasons why this might be so, and why free trade relations, which have been discussed between Canada and the United States since at least 1920, have suddenly become a reality, or, in Mexico's case, we feel are moving rapidly toward reality.

One possible reason for these closer relations is the global climate. No one can deny the enormous progress that has been made, largely through GATT, toward a much more open world trade system since the last war. However, now there is also a very real nervousness abroad about the possible shape of future world trade. In particular these fears revolve around the emergence of gigantic trading blocs such as the European Community (especially with a united Germany and the prospect of Eastern Europe being brokered in after 1992), and some possible East Asian group with its potential trade alliances built around Japan.

Relatively small economies such as Canada and Mexico, measured on the world scale, face the very real possibility—in the absence of any guarantees—of being locked out of the European and East Asian blocs. At the same time, the United States could face the prospect of being sandwiched between two giant blocs, while it sees its economic and political world-power status slipping away. One way of reducing the imagined negative effects of this situation would be an element of bloc-formation within the hemisphere. To this end, closer economic ties may be seen as a response to a rapidly changing world scene that renders all the earlier assumptions less valid, if not inoperative. Not everyone will agree with this, but it seems to be at least one very significant conclusion that can be drawn from the available evidence. It may also be argued, along these lines, that the growing tendency to interact with the US market leaves these two neighbors in an extremely vulnerable position if there is not some formalization of the economic relationship among them. Their success might well lead to focussed US retaliation, through protectionism, in the absence of a broad consensus, or a "shared vision," to use a term we have liberally adopted from the Bilateral Commission on US-Mexican relations. To have to confront a world of trading blocs, *and* growing protectionism within the United States, would leave these countries in a very exposed position indeed.

We also wish to stress several other underlying assumptions that seem of great practical value to us. The first of these is that the future form, pace, and nature of change in the economic relations among these countries is likely to be influenced by global economics, perceived political expediency, and the extraordinary speed with which the old world is unravelling. As in Europe, it may well be the case that broad goals will be set by inevitability, and the machinery will have to follow (e.g., 1992). A second point to be stressed is that this paper does not explore, to any significant depth, the theory of free trade agreements, trade creation/diversion etc. A broad, and accessible, literature on the basic theory is available, and some of it is referred to in the following text. However, experience seems to suggest that these technical and theoretical aspects are often of significance in adjusting, or detailing, elements of a relationship, not in initiating one.

There is a third consideration which has weighed heavily with us. That is the growing realization that the past offers little in the way of lessons for the future, especially as the pace of change itself seems to be accelerating so powerfully. While not advocating Henry Ford's dictum that "history is bunk," we agree with Paul Kennedy who has pointed out (1988), that there really is no historical precedent for the world in which we now live. The traditional definition of great power status is horribly confused by today's "multi-polar" and rapidly globalizing situation. It is very easy to sit back and look at the cultural, historical, economic, political, and other differences between the United States and Mexico, and to say "Canadian-Mexican-US economic community"—it can never happen." Or, "not in my lifetime." We should remember that we have seen, in recent years, the sudden evaporation of the "Thousand-Year Reich," the eclipse of "The Empire on which the sun never sets," the restoration of democracy to the "workers' states," and Nelson Mandela at the independence celebrations for Namibia—and much more. This is no time to make bold assumptions based on the past. The players in today's world are moving about the field trying to find out what happened to the rules, and where the "other side" went. So, we offer no apologies for thinking the unthinkable. At the same time, we do not deny the many attitudes, perceptions, and even neuroses that have served to separate the neighbors on the North American continent up to now. Our point is that, today, there are greater imperatives.

Canadian-US Economic Interdependence 1935-88

The US-Canada Free Trade Agreement (FTA) of 1989 is best understood in the context of industrial and trade development between the two countries over the past half-century. From the nadir in the early 1930s, with the Smoot-Hawley Tariff Act and Canadian retaliation, relations began to improve in 1935 with a trade agreement, which was enlarged in 1938, to initiate the process of tariff reduction. Soon after World War II, a free trade agreement was discussed, but the Liberal government of MacKenzie King cautiously rejected the proposal in favor of GATT negotiations to lower trade barriers. In the 1950s the Conservatives, led by John Diefenbaker, promoted closer ties with Great Britain; and in the 1970s, the Liberals, under Pierre Elliott Trudeau, sought expanded trade with the European Community. Despite these efforts, Canadian exports to the United States have continued to grow, rising from 55.9% of total exports in 1958 to 70.3% in 1978, while exports to the UK have fallen from 17.4% in 1958 to 3.8% in 1978 and somewhat less in 1988, and exports to the EC declined from 13.1% in 1980 to 6.5% in 1988 as seen in Figure 2.1.

Today, by far the largest component of Canadian-US trade is the auto sector, with about $50 billion or one-third of bilateral merchandise trade. In the early 1960s, however, this trade accounted for less than 4% of bilateral trade or less than one billion dollars. Its dramatic growth has resulted from the only major trade agreement between the two countries between 1935 and 1988, the US-Canadian Agreement Concerning Automotive Products of 1965. The Auto Pact was negotiated to resolve a dispute between US auto parts manufacturers and the Canadian government, concerning the latter's duty remission program that the US manufacturers claimed was an illegal subsidy to Canadian exporters. To reduce its automobile trade deficit and encourage greater growth and efficiency of its auto industry, in the early

Figure 2.1 Canadian Exports to the United States, the United Kingdom, and the European Community as Percentages of Total Canadian Exports, 1953-1989

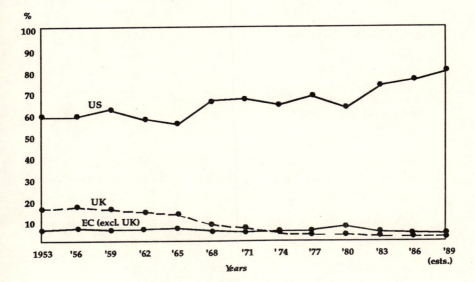

Source: Canada Yearbook; *Historical Statistics of Canada,* 2nd ed.

1960s the Canadian government had unilaterally instituted a change in policy to allow Canadian manufacturers duty remissions on imported vehicles or original equipment components if matched by exports on any vehicle or part. When the United States challenged this scheme in 1964, the Canadian and US governments negotiated the Auto Pact, which permits duty-free treatment to imports of specified automotive products that originate in either country. In the case of Canadian exports, however, the Canadian firms must produce approximately as many cars in Canada as they sell there and achieve a Canadian value-added greater than 60% of the value of the cars sold in Canada (Wonnacott 1988: 102). These "special safeguards" favoring Canadian producers are one source of disagreement that is addressed in the FTA.

The accession of the United Kingdom to the European Community in 1973 meant that Canada lost its privileged access to the British market accorded Commonwealth members and became a disadvantaged outsider facing the EC's common external tariff. As Little has noted, this significant change

> underscored Canada's vulnerable position as one of the few industrialized countries without unimpeded and secure access to a market of one hundred million or more customers. The US and Japan both have large domestic markets, and the Europeans trade tariff-free within the EC common market and European Free Trade Area. To make matters worse from the Canadian perspective, access to the US market has become progressively less assured (Little 1988: 4).

In the 1970s, the OPEC embargo exacerbated trade tensions and contributed to increased protectionism. Some of the actions taken by the Canadian and US governments affecting bilateral trade in energy were as follows:

- Canada temporarily cut exports of oil to the US at the time of the Arab embargo in the early 1970s when shortages were occurring throughout the United States.

- The US mandatory oil import quota from 1958 to 1973 was implemented in a manner that prevented increased Canadian exports to the US through "informal advice."

- Canada adopted an energy plan in the late 1970s that sought to terminate exports to the US by the early 1980s.

- US government controls on the wellhead price of natural gas held prices below market levels, effectively denying Canadian exports access to the US market.

- Canada pursued a program to reduce foreign investment in its energy industries.

- The US denied potentially lower-cost Alaskan crude oil to west coast Canadian refiners, forcing them to purchase more expensive supplies.

- Canada imposed a system of export taxes and export price controls that ensured that US consumers paid much higher prices than did Canadian consumers.

- The US proposed and then abandoned a pipeline to bring natural gas from Alaska to the lower 48 states after encouraging the Canadians to start construction on the Canadian portion (Verleger 1988: 177-8).

Although the FTA enhances US energy supply assurances and eliminates most border restraints and minimum price requirements, it falls far short of effectively encouraging the long-run development of Canadian energy resources because it continues Canadian ownership restrictions (further below).

In the early 1970s, concern about the power and influence of foreign-owned business led the Canadian government to promulgate the Foreign Investment Review Act (FIRA). Foreign firms, primarily US companies, held controlling interests in approximately 75% of the petroleum industry and 60% of mining and manufacturing industries in Canada. Under FIRA requirements in the 1970s, direct and indirect takeovers as well as new businesses set up by foreign firms were subject to review to determine whether the foreign acquisitions "significantly benefitted" Canada. As part of the review process, the foreign firms "were often encouraged to make undertakings about import and export performance, employment, local sourcing of inputs, research and development efforts, and investment plans" (Schott and Smith 1988: 146). FIRA regulations were strengthened in the early 1980s under the Liberal government of Pierre Elliott Trudeau, which introduced the National Energy Program of taxes and subsidies that discriminated against in foreign energy companies. Tensions reached a conflict with the US government's protest and subsequent complaint under the GATT about FIRA performance requirements. The GATT ruling, accepted by the Canadian government, was that the export performance requirements violated no GATT rules, but the obligations imposed on firms concerning domestic sourcing of goods were contrary to the international treaty.

US and other foreign investment is less controversial in Canada today, although the FTA perpetuates many of Canada's energy ownership restrictions and some controls over takeovers of large Canadian firms. In the 1980s Canadian direct investment in the United States grew much faster than US investment in Canada, so that by 1988 total US investments in Canada were only about two times larger than Canadian investments in the US, in contrast to ten times larger in the early 1970s. Further, research by Alan Rugman (1988: 181-98) reveals that US subsidiaries in Canada export about one-quarter of their output on average and Canadian subsidiaries in the US purchase on average five times as much from their parent firms in Canada as they export back to Canada. For the 1975-84 period, Rugman found that Canada had maintained a net surplus ranging from $2.1 to $4.3 billion on the multinational enterprise trade.

Impetus for the Free Trade Agreement

In 1984, Canadian voters rejected the Liberal government and its National Energy Program in favor of the Progressive Conservative government of Brian Mulroney. The Foreign Investment Review Act was renamed Investment Canada, review of new businesses was stopped (except in publishing and film distribution where restrictions were increased), and thresholds of C$5 million and C$50 million were established for the review of direct and indirect acquisitions (Schott and Smith 1988: 147). Even before the election, however, the recession of 1980-82 and collapse of oil prices had prompted Pierre Elliott Trudeau's Liberal government to take a more conciliatory policy toward foreign investment and to propose trade talks with the US on obtaining access to the US petrochemical market and public procurement for urban transit vehicles, matters that were not resolved in the Tokyo Round under the GATT. The US accepted the Canadian invitation, but the talks failed because US objectives differed widely (Hufbauer and Samet 1985: 96).

The failure of these bilateral negotiations in 1983 and the earlier disappointing results of the GATT ministerial meetings in 1982 underscored US determination to reach an agreement with Canada, pre-negotiations for which were announced at the "Shamrock" Summit meeting of President Ronald Reagan and Prime Minister Brian Mulroney in Quebec on March 17, 1985. The United States had tried in the early 1980s to initiate a new round of multilateral trade negotiations under the GATT, especially in the areas of trade-related investment, intellectual property and services, but the failure of the 1982 GATT ministerial meeting led to bilateral initiatives with Caribbean countries, Israel (culminating in a Free Trade Agreement in 1985), and Canada. US trade negotiators wanted to prove that progress in liberalizing trade was possible, and to hold up some bilateral agreements as models in the Uruguay Round of GATT negotiations.

As trade deficits increased and protectionist pressures rose in the mid-1980s, there was also greater pressure to apply unfair trade laws and to fall back on orderly marketing arrangements and voluntary export restraints.

Both countries were motivated to develop a new trade agreement to avoid disputes and the imposition of protectionist measures that disrupt trade. To be sure, the United States and Canada have been at odds over trade disputes for almost as long as they have engaged in international trade. In recent years, however, the frequency of disputes has increased and the dollar amounts of trade at stake have risen dramatically. Since 1980, the United States has imposed countervailing duties against Canadian exporters in six instances and antidumping penalties in nine cases; Canada has acted once against US exporters with countervailing duties and 23 times with antidumping penalties (Horlick, Oliver and Steger 1988: 81). Also, over time both governments have widened their definitions of dumping and subsidy. For example, the United States originally limited its definition of subsidy to measures specifically designed to promote exports, but in 1973 broadened the scope of the term to include a Canadian government grant that was intended primarily to stimulate regional economic development (Wonnacott 1987: 23).

From Canada's point of view, the rise in US protectionism in the 1980s rekindled old fears of losing access to the large US market. Nearly 30 years ago, the Bladen Report made it clear to Canadian producers that they would remain small and inefficient, unable to compete in world markets, as long as they were confined to the small, protected Canadian market. The antidumping and countervailing duty cases, as well as other US protectionist measures, made access to the US market less certain, and thus deterred Canadian firms from investing in Canada and, importantly, in plants of world-class size and efficiency.

> Instead, protected by Canada's relatively high tariffs and thwarted by actual and contingent trade barriers in the United States, Canadian manufacturers focus on the domestic market and supply the whole range of products within each industry. As a result, in many industries, Canada has a plethora of small plants producing too many products in short, fragmented production runs (Little 1988: 5).

Even though the Canadian market is only one-tenth the size of the US market, Canada is the United States' largest trading partner, receiving 21% of US exports, almost two times greater than Japanese exports, the second largest. Since Canadian tariffs are relatively high, on average 9.9% on dutiable US imports (in contrast with US tariffs, which average 3.3%) (Schott 1988: 15), elimination of tariffs under a free trade agreement was particularly attractive to US exporters. This trade-weighted average masks the deterrent effect of the many much higher tariffs, e.g., on textiles, clothing and footwear (from 20 to 25%), rubber gloves (25%), and telephone sets (17.5%). The removal of tariffs on such products is likely to create new export opportunities for US manufacturers of products that have been effectively shut out of Canadian markets.

Provisions and Expected Effects of the FTA

Under the Free Trade Agreement, which was signed by President Reagan and Prime Minister Mulroney on January 2, 1988 and ratified by the US Senate on September 19, 1988 and the Canadian Parliament in December 1988, all tariffs between the two countries will be eliminated by January 1, 1998. Some tariffs will be eliminated immediately, but most will be phased out in five to ten years in equal annual installments. Also eliminated will be virtually all quotas, embargoes, and minimum price requirements. The major exceptions are agricultural quotas and price support or subsidy programs and restrictions on log exports of both countries; Canadian protective regulations on the sale and distribution of beer (but discriminatory pricing of distilled spirits and wine will be phased out); restrictions on energy products as permitted by the GATT for shortages, conservation and national security; Canadian regulations protecting books, magazines, newspapers, films, video and audio recordings, and broadcasting; and government procurement preferences not covered by GATT. In cases in which traded products are made from parts or materials imported from countries other than Canada or the United States, the rules of origin of the FTA provide that the products must have sufficient value added (for autos, 50% of direct manufacturing costs) within either country to permit them to be exported under a tariff classification different from that of the imported components. Except for apparel products made of imported fabrics, on which the FTA establishes quotas for tariff-free treatment, duty drawbacks (refunds of tariffs paid on imported parts or materials when the final products are exported) and customs users' fees will be eliminated on January 1, 1994.

Estimates of the economic impact of the removal of tariffs range from large gains (9% of real GNP, Harris 1985: 173) to small losses (0.4%, Brown and Stern 1987: 209) in Canadian real income, and from small gains (0.03%, Hamilton and Whalley 1985: 449) to small losses (0.02%, Hill and Whalley 1985: 265) in US real income. As with all econometric methods, the results of these studies depend critically on their underlying assumptions. The studies which assume that economies of large-scale production are not significant and markets are competitive tend to find that the gains from bilateral free trade will be quite small for each country, less than 1 or 2% of GNP. On the other hand, research that assumes that economies of scale are important and markets are oligopolistic or monopolistic usually shows much larger welfare gains from free trade. For example, Harris and Cox (1985) used estimates of scale economies from previous econometric studies and engineering work to reach the conclusion that *multilateral* free trade would increase Canadian real income by 8 to 9% of GNP. Even though the Harris-Cox research was one of the most detailed and comprehensive studies of the effect of the FTA, and is based on a major general equilibrium model, it has been criticized for not using independent estimates of scale economies. Wonnacott (1987: 32) observes that the estimates of scale economies used by Harris and Cox were probably upwardly biased, and thus the gains from free trade will be smaller. Little (1988: 12) argues that Canadian gains from the bilateral FTA are likely to be 2 or 3% of GNP under the Harris-Cox model when more recent data on lower tariff rates are used (Harris and Cox used pre-Tokyo Round tariffs), as well as more conservative estimates of economies of scale, monopolistic pricing, and elasticities of demand.

If, as most research agrees, the elimination of tariffs under the FTA will lead to at least modest welfare gains for both countries from trade creation and expansion, will it also cause welfare losses from trade diversion? Such losses may occur as the result of the displacement of a lower-cost third country's exports, burdened by tariffs, by Canada's or the United States' duty-free exports to the other. Trade diversion losses are not likely to be great because each country has been the other's largest export market by far, tariff rates for the past decade have been quite low, and both countries' exports compete with products from the EC or EFTA, which already discriminate against the US and Canada. To the extent that trade diversion results in welfare losses, the problem would appear to mainly affect developing countries, particularly producers of steel, replacement auto parts, textiles, and apparel.

Although the FTA may result in real income increases and improvements in economic efficiency in the long run, it may also cause short-run costs of dislocations necessitating adjustments. Wonnacott (1987: 33) distinguishes two types of adjustments:

1. adjustment *within* industries, particularly in Canada, as plants and firms specialize for the larger US-Canada market; and
2. adjustment *between* industries, as the United States tends to specialize in some products and Canada in others (Wonnacott 1987: 33).

Free trade will result in greater specialization and larger-scale plants, hence intra-industry adjustments, particularly in the smaller Canadian plants, will require reorganization and less diversity in products manufactured. Inter-industry adjustments will probably be more disruptive, requiring retraining or relocation of workers. Research by Brown and Stern (1987), Harris, (1985) and Magun (1986) suggests that in Canada the chemicals, electrical equipment, financial services, furniture, leather and leather products, and metal fabrication industries are the most likely to suffer decreases in production as a result of free trade. In the United States, the most vulnerable industries include paper and paper products, machinery, petroleum products, and transportation equipment. In the apparel and textiles industries, greater specialization and increased economies of scale under the FTA should strengthen US and Canadian industries, both under attack from strong competition overseas, but most of the adjustment will be within, not between industries. In the steel industry, the large integrated Canadian firms have been generally healthier and less vulnerable to Japanese and European competition than the traditional US companies, which have also been hurt by much lower domestic demand than anticipated and have lost market share to new US mini-mills. Crandall (1987) predicts, however, that the US industry will not lose much market share to the Canadian steel firms, because labor costs in Canada have been rising much faster than in the US It should be noted also that the US and Canadian steel companies have a gentlemen's agreement to limit Canadian exports.

There are many other non-tariff barriers between Canada and the United States, only a few of which are affected by the FTA. Magun, Rao, and Lodh (1988) calculated the tariff equivalents of many of these NTBs but concluded that the FTA will leave most of them intact. For example, under the FTA the contract-value threshold of government procurement bids available to firms in either country will fall from $171,000 to $25,000, potentially opening up new trading opportunities. However, as Magun, Rao, and Lodh (1988) point out, informal practices will continue to discriminate in favor of national suppliers, subnational governments are not covered by the FTA, and services are also excluded. The result is that government procurement provisions of the FTA will have little effect on trade, output, or employment. Another sector that has been protected by NTBs is energy, particularly natural gas (5.3% of US consumption imported from Canada in 1985), oil (3.6%, although Canada is the United States' largest foreign supplier), and electricity (1.8%). On the positive side, the FTA outlaws import or export barriers, including quotas, taxes or price requirements, except for military needs in times of national security or short supplies (when supplies must be shared proportionately between the two countries). However, as Verleger points out, the FTA is

> of very marginal importance because it fails to address the vital long-term issue of development of Canadian energy supplies. In fact, the agreement sanctions the continuation of a Canadian investment policy that explicitly favors Canadian companies. US acquiescence on this point is deplorable, both because the Canadian approach has contributed to an unnecessary increase in dependence by major industrialized countries on insecure supplies of oil from the Middle East and because acceptance of bad Canadian policies weakens the United States' ability to oppose bad policies such as import fees in the United States (Verleger 1988: 118-9).

In natural gas the FTA will have only a limited effect on Canada's ability to increase its access to the US market because regulations in the two countries are incompatible, the US being mainly unregulated and Canada not. Some of the barriers to Canadian electricity exports will be removed by the FTA, but Canada's National Energy Board will continue its authority to limit exports unless they are certified to be surplus to Canada's needs.

In sectors other than energy, the FTA improves the investment climate in Canada by phasing out within three years most of the screening requirements that apply to new businesses (greenfield investments) and indirect acquisitions by US firms, and by raising the threshold for screening of direct acquisitions to C$150 million from the present C$5 million threshold. Also, under the FTA, new trade-related performance requirements, which were used to discourage foreign investment, will be outlawed. However, non-trade related performance requirements (e.g., employment or training) may still be imposed, and screening will continue on US investments in companies that hold large market shares in Canada. In practical terms, screening will apply to the direct acquisitions of approximately the largest 600 non-financial companies and to grandfathered sectors (e.g., energy) (Schott and Smith 1988: 148). Minimum Canadian equity requirements, although barred for the future, are also grandfathered in specified industries.

US banks, trust and loan companies, and insurance companies, largely excluded from Canada in the past by restrictions on market share, asset ownership, and capital expansion, will enjoy much greater access under the FTA. US commercial banks operating in Canada prior to the agreement will no longer be subject to most of the restrictions on foreign firms, and new US entrants will be treated as Canadian applicants. Similar restrictions will also be removed for US insurance, trust, and loan companies. Canadian financial institutions have generally enjoyed freer access to US markets, and the FTA guarantees these rights and protects them against discriminatory treatment in the event that US laws are changed.

Almost all existing restrictions on trade in non-financial services (except transportation services, which are excluded from the FTA, and most government and social services) are grandfathered under the FTA. For the most part, however, these restrictions have not seriously limited trade nor led to major disputes, and the FTA imposes an obligation on federal, state and local governments of each country not to enact new laws or regulations that would distort bilateral service transactions or discriminate against service firms from the other country. As Schott and Smith observe, "national treatment is the norm; where it is not applicable, the differential treatment of foreign firms should not involve implicit protection for domestic firms" (1988: 140). To ensure that national treatment has meaning, the FTA guarantees rights of commercial access through establishment of a business or use of distribution channels. In addition to these general provisions, there are four sectoral annexes in the FTA, covering architecture, tourism, computer services, and telecommunications. Going beyond the standstill principle, each sectoral annex aims to initiate further negotiations on common regulatory standards and to roll back existing restrictions.

Finally, the FTA establishes a Canada-US Trade Commission to administer the agreement and to adjudicate disputes arising under it, except disputes concerning antidumping, countervailing duties, and financial services. Each country will continue to enforce its own countervailing duty and antidumping laws, subject to review by a special binational panel, and disputes on financial services will be administered by the US Treasury and the Canadian Department of Finance. In general matters under the FTA, the Commission must first try to diffuse potential disputes by setting up consultations between the interested parties and experts, to clarify interpretation of proposed new laws or rules. When disputes occur, the Commission follows procedures to resolve them that are much less time-consuming than either national process or under the GATT. A new body of Canadian-US trade law should gradually emerge, which will replace the separate national laws and thus facilitate dispute resolution and strengthen bilateral cooperation.

Appraisal of the Free Trade Agreement

The expected gains and losses of the FTA were more extensively debated in Canada than in the United States. Given the relative size of the countries and the likely greater impact of the agreement on Canada, it is not surprising that Canadians were more concerned. As former Prime Minister Pierre Elliott Trudeau once reminded a US audience, "Living next to you is in some ways like sleeping with an elephant: no matter how friendly and even-tempered the beast, one is affected by every twitch and grunt" (Trudeau 1982). Even though President Reagan placed his considerable personal support behind the FTA, the US elephant lumbered on, largely unworried about its effects. In contrast, Canadians made the FTA the central issue of a national election in the fall of 1988,

> the most fundamental decision on national identity that the country could likely make for the remainder of the century—an issue, as such critics as Robertson Davies saw it, of whether the government was "signing away Canada's soul" (McDonald 1989: 28).

Throughout the campaign public opinion pools showed strong support for free trade, at the same time that Canadians were reasserting their national distinctiveness. For example, a survey of 1,000 persons of each nationality found that 43% of Canadians versus 21% of Americans described Canadians and Americans as "mainly or essentially different." Eighty-five percent of the Canadians surveyed, as opposed to 32% of the US respondents, strongly opposed or opposed Canada becoming the 51st state of the United States, and 49% of the Canadians versus 23% of the Americans opposed or strongly opposed Canada and the United States adopting a common currency (*Maclean's* 1989: 49-50).

On three previous occasions in Canadian history, free trade was rejected, but in November 1988 it won decisive approval. Mulroney's Progressive Conservatives won 170 (or 57.6%) of the 295 seats in the House of Commons, which was, however, 40 fewer than in the 1984 election that brought the Conservatives to power and less than half of the popular vote. The Prime Minister's main strength was in Quebec, where support for the FTA was greatest (as, indeed, public opinion has favored a common currency and political union with the United States much more than in other provinces of Canada). Even in Ontario, which was the center of opposition to the FTA, the Conservatives won 47 of the 99 seats. In all of Canada, the Liberals who attacked the FTA won 82 seats (27.8%) and the socialist New Democrats secured 43 seats (14.6%).

Political analysts will discuss the Canadian election for years to come, but we suggest that there were two overriding reasons for the acceptance of the FTA. The first is defensive, "to provide Canada with insurance against the risk that the protectionist tide in America will provide irresistible after President Reagan, a defender of free trade, vacates the White House" (*Economist* 1988: Survey Canada 8). Canadians remember all too well the devastating effect of Nixon's surprise 10% surcharge on all US imports in 1971, and US countervailing or antidumping duty cases against Canadian exporters are front-page news in Canada. Because 75-80% of Canadian exports go to the United States and these exports account for nearly 20% of Canada's GNP, US import restrictions that seem minor to Americans usually have significant and adverse impacts in Canada. The Tokyo Round of tariff reductions since the late 1970s has benefitted Canada; Canadian economic growth in the 1980s has been among the highest of the OECD countries. Canadians realize that access to the largest, most affluent market in the world has contributed in no small part to their greater efficiency and prosperity, and that the FTA will help assure continued access to this market.

The second set of factors that explain the Canadian approval of the FTA refers to the strengthening of the "fiber of Canadian nationhood by helping to equalize economic opportunity in Canada" (Macdonald Royal Commission 1985: Vol. 1, 138). The fear of being taken over by the United States manifests itself from time to time in Canada, as for example, the Foreign Investment Review Agency (FIRA) in the mid-1970s and the National Energy Program of the early 1980s. Some of the same nationalist sentiments recur in the Free Trade Agreement, for example, to protect Canada's cultural identity, US imports or production of books, magazines, newspapers, films, video and audio recordings and broadcasting are excluded from the agreement. Overall, however, Canadian voters rejected the argument that the FTA would destroy Canadian sovereignty.

> And are the critics not forgetting Canadian history and the very significant social, economic, philosophical, and institutional differences that distinguish Canadians from Americans? In time, some of these differences will soften, others will become more pronounced. Of one thing we can be certain, however: political will alone will not guarantee Canadian sovereignty. Political will combined with economic strength, on the other hand, will allow us as a people to continue the job of nation building without fear of domination from any quarter (d'Aquino 1988: 57).

An isolationist Canada (or the United States) would be weaker and more vulnerable to dissension from within and takeover from the outside. The FTA provides the opportunity and discipline to become stronger economically, hence to maintain political integrity.

In the United States debate over the FTA occurred mainly among business people who had consulted with the trade negotiators and in the US Senate which ratified the treaty in September 1988, two months before the Canadian election. Thus, issues in the United States were more specific to particular industries affected. For example, US auto parts manufacturers argued for increased protection against competition from overseas suppliers, and they won a partial victory in the FTA rule of origin formula that effectively increases the amount of US and Canadian parts required. The entire transportation sector was excluded from the draft agreement after the US maritime industry succeeded in forcing the deletion of provisions that would have exempted Canada from future changes in US maritime restrictions (Schott 1988: 13). US plywood manufacturers complained that Canadian construction standards will disqualify most US plywood in housing financed by the Canada Housing and Mortgage Corporation. The FTA compromise is an attachment that provides that Canada will review the standards and, if they are not liberalized, the US tariff on plywood will remain in force (Little 1988: 16).

From the US point of view, the FTA failed to achieve a number of desired concessions from the Canadians. Perhaps the most important of these shortcomings is the failure to agree on new rules governing the use of domestic subsidies. The parties agreed only to continue negotiations on this issue, with the result that disputes, for example, as to whether investment incentives are illegal will continue to be resolved under each country's countervailing or antidumping duty laws. A second major disappointment is the failure of the FTA to reduce the restrictions on foreign ownership in Canada's energy industries. By allowing the Canadians to keep these restrictions, the US negotiators failed to encourage the much-needed long-term development of Canadian energy supplies.

The Origins of Mexican Industrial Development

It is quite impossible to consider prospects or models for closer integration between Mexico, the United States, and Canada, without an understanding of the context within which Mexico's modernization took place. This process will be covered in this section; the next section looks at how this has changed, particularly since the mid-1980s.

Mexican industrialization dates back to the 1920s, but the main thrust occurred from about 1940. However, the policy climate within which this growth occurred as very different from that of its northern neighbor:

> Since coming to power in 1929. the Institutional Revolutionary Party has emphasized development of the Mexican economy by keeping foreign competition out and subsidizing domestic producers. This model was developed in large part to prevent Mexico and its economy from being swallowed by US interests, whose extensive acquisition of mines, railroads, oil companies and ranches helped detonate the revolution that the party still claims to defend (Rohter 1990).

Writing in 1981, Purcell summarized Mexico's industrialization as follows:

> Mexico's impressive level of industrialization dates from the 1940s, and owes much to the effort of the state to protect and nurture Mexican industry from foreign competition. Tariffs, import quotas and licenses, and government subsidies were, and continue to be, the main tools used to encourage Mexican industrial development (Purcell 1981: 385).

The pattern of Mexico's industrial development was very much aligned to the import-substitution, rather than the export-led, model. In addition to the instruments mentioned by Purcell, there was also a strict foreign-investment code guaranteeing Mexico a 51% stake in any foreign enterprise developed in the country. Isolating the nascent industries from competition, and financially insulating them with public subsidies led to a situation evaluated by Luis Rubio in the following terms:

> Foreign trade has been managed, since the 1960s, essentially through import quotas controlled by import permits. These quotas have been used either to ban imports or to direct industrial production. Though the original purpose of this policy was to promote development of a competitive domestic industrial base over the years, excessive protection has led to inefficiency, inflexibility and incapacity to generate exports (Luis Rubio 1987: 18).

Expansion of industry remained a problem because, again as Luis Rubio noted, the domestic market was too small to support an economic scale of operation which could be transferred into something competitive on the global, or international, market place. Furthermore, the absence of competition meant that the quality of product, and the need to keep at the forefront of technology, had been largely neglected. This meant that foreign exchange earnings relied on a largely "Third World" pattern of selling agricultural products, some tourism, and a little labor-intensive industry. By 1982 the Mexican state sector controlled an estimated 65% of the economy, and had established over 1,100 parastatal enterprises covering utilities, production, and distribution areas.

If anything, this situation was worsened by the development of Mexico's oil industry. This grew astonishingly from 420 million bbl. in 1976 to 15 *billion* bbl. in 1982, which was also a time of extraordinary price increases (Gilbreath 1986: 10). By 1985 oil had come to account for about 90% of Mexico's export earnings. This change had two major effects on the existing policy: it generated vast public funds to further protected industrialization, and it gave the country the apparent financial capacity to borrow heavily on the commercial markets against "future earnings" from oil, based on simple projections of the past revenues. So, by 1986, looking back on the experience of 40 years, Castenada lamented:

> Whether for businessmen or economic planners, the Mexican economy has been turned into a nightmare by . . . protectionism, inefficiency, massive subsidization of both consumer staples and industrial inputs, and technological backwardness. [Protectionism] created a national industry which generally produces poor-quality and high-priced goods, which is totally unprepared for export-oriented growth, and which has developed a yawning technological gap (Castenada 1986: 296-297).

Because of its essentially uncompetitive nature, except for typical "Third World" primary goods and oil, Mexican industry relied heavily on special concessions to enter the United States market, such as the Generalized System of Preferences usually reserved for less-developed countries.

The non-productive, and uncompetitive nature of much of the public borrowing and spending came home to roost dramatically in 1982 with the announcement that Mexico would not be able to service its debt payments, along with the accompanying international nightmare of default which became the eternal bogeyman lurking around every turn along Mexico's path to real change and development.

The immediate response to 1982 by the government of Mexico was sudden and drastic. A program of austerity, import restrictions, and major cuts in public expenditure was introduced, an 80% devaluation of the peso took place (causing unemployment on the United States side of the border to rise by 30% [Weintraub 1986: 4]), and deflation and tighter exchange controls prevailed. These, plus the (perceived) nightmare of the debt overhang, led to a serious lack of confidence which, in turn, led to massive capital flight estimated at possibly $50 billion (Castenada 1986: 296), at a time when the government was having to induce lenders to lend more to cover interest payment on the foreign debt. The government, in an attempt to gain greater control of the runaway situation, nationalized the banks in 1982, further fuelling the crisis of confidence. This negative view of the country's future by the middle and working classes was driven home by a fall in the economic growth rate by 12.6% to *minus* 4.7% in the year following the harsh measures. Those with money sent it abroad "to buy back the southwest" (Weintraub 1986: 9); those without took off across the international border, so that, by 1986, estimates of Mexican "illegals" in the United States were placed at between six and twelve million (Gilbreath 1986: 13). Job creation dried up between 1982 and 1986 in a country that has to find 800,000 new positions annually just to keep up with the natural increase in the population (Castenada 1986: 295).

Things continued to get worse as Mexico's principal foreign revenue earner, oil, was severely depressed by the fall in oil prices in the mid-1980s. The country's capacity to repay its debts was thereby reduced further, while the debts themselves were increased sharply by the rising value of the US dollar, and United States interest rates which were pegged at a level to cover the Federal need for money to cover deficit financing. So, although by 1986 some relaxation was possible as a result of the impressive Mexican response to the austerity package (particularly restricting imports), another recession threatened (Williamson 1990: 45). In part this was due to depressed domestic demand arising from falling oil revenues and declining real wage rates (Trigueros 1989: 260). In 1986 Mexico registered a 4% decline in growth, a 10.7% reduction in gross fixed investment, a 3.8% decline in manufacturing activity, and the loss of 1.5 million jobs. "In this climate Mexico refused to accept a decrease in imports or government spending, continual currency devaluation, recession and inflation" (Kreinin 1981: 32). The economic program was running onto the political rocks. In a feature on "The economic crisis in Mexico," Comercio commented:

> After some four years of great sacrifices, we find ourselves today in the same spot, with inflation expected to reach its highest level since 1982, productivity, again, falling severely, and the financial deficit of the public sector continuing unabated. We have regressed in social welfare. The purchasing power of the minimum wage continues falling behind. We are on the verge of repeating the 1983 severe fall of the productive sector. . . . We are back again, at the inflation-devaluation-recession cycle (*Comercio* 28, No.36 March 1987: 7).

The purpose of this protracted account of the last 40 years of Mexican development is to stress the really remarkable efforts made by the country, not just to combat the dead hand of 1982, but to rethink fundamentally the established foundations upon which the Mexican industrial development program was built.

Recent Changes in the Mexican Economy and Trade Climate

Prior to 1986 it would have been difficult to envisage closer links between Mexico and the United States, as the contrast between a managed economy and an open one was extremely stark. However, the changes over the last few years have radically altered the prospects and realities of closer cooperation. The Mexican economy is now characterized by much greater openness and a trend toward export-led growth rather than the typical inward-looking approach of the last half-century.

The de la Madrid, and later, Salinas governments have pushed through a whole package of reforms in the areas of trade and economic relations. Some of these relate to the more global perspective of the two leaders, some to the ministrations of the IMF in conjunction with their recommended restructuring. This was reflected in the "Solidarity Pact" put in place in December 1987 that included "wage and price controls and an initial freeze (followed by a gradual crawl) of the exchange rate, which brought down the inflation rate to about 20 percent per year" (Williamson 1990: 46). The reduction in inflation and some recovery by the peso helped to reduce, and to some extent turn around, capital flight. By the last quarter of 1988 the inflation rate was down to 15%, compared with 224% in the last quarter of 1987 (Inter-American Development Bank 1989: 18).

The other reforms have been very comprehensive. The state initiated a program of disengagement and privatization so that by 1989 "about 130 mostly small state enterprises have so far been privatized, and only 496 [376 by March 1990] of the 1,155 state enterprises existing in 1983 are still state owned. The process is proceeding, with the telephone company a leading candidate. Limited private competition is now allowed in some petrochemicals" (Williamson 1990: 29). Related progress has been made in the context of deregulation, especially in the transportation sector. With regard to the area of import duties, tariffs and import licensing—the shield behind which Mexican protectionism for so long remained sheltered—the changes have been profound. The import licensing system was virtually abolished in 1989, removing a major bureaucratic obstruction to the free flow of trade. This is in contrast to 1985 when the system still covered 95% of imports. At the same time the Mexican government has cut tariffs, which until recently had been at least twice as high as their equivalents in the United States, to an average (spring 1990) weighted rate of 6.2% or less. Previously the only real import duty relief was applied to the foreign ventures operating in the *maquiladora* (export processing) zone along the United States border. Quotas were reduced drastically, including—in early 1990—those on textiles, steel, and apparel. A major related event was the decision, taken by Mexico in 1986, to join the General Agreement on Tariffs and Trade (GATT)—a move replete with serious implications in the light of the current Uruguay Round which covers agriculture and subsidies. This would have been largely unthinkable for the Mexico of the 1970s since it would have been in direct contradiction to the nations' protectionist, interventionist stance. This decision, as much as anything, indicates the changed direction of Mexican thinking regarding trade and the prospects for changed relations with its neighbor to the north, and with the rest of the world.

Concurrent with the above came a freeing up of the regulations restricting foreign investment in May 1989. This has not been generalized yet but offers a major area of relief from the 51% Mexican partnership requirement that had previously been in place. The need for investment is so great that liberalization seems inevitable. Undercapitalization has been a major constraint on responsiveness in the Mexican oil industry recently. In the bilateral field the new openness was a major factor in the ability of the United States and Mexico to negotiate a Framework Agreement in November 1987 which set up "a bilateral forum in which some of the most nettlesome trade disputes are being addressed, many for the first time" (Kolbe 1988: 14). This Agreement has since been converted into a mechanism "for negotiating ways of increasing trade and investment. This undramatic action could pave the way for big changes" (*Economist* 1989b: 28). The Americans further agreed to give preferential tariff treatment to 43 items on a Mexican list of 63.

The general turn around of economic posture can be seen in the fact that non-oil exports to the United States have grown from $3.5 billion in 1980 to $10.4 billion in 1987, the share of manufactures as a percentage of total exports rising from 22% to 48% over the same period (Bilateral Commission 1989: 43), though, to be fair, it should be noted that the draconian measures of 1982 began this trend, so that from 1982-86 exports of manufactures from Mexico to the United States grew 28% annually displacing oil as the principal traded item in 1986 (see Figure 2.2).

In 1988, for the third consecutive year, manufacturing exports showed a real growth rate in excess of 10%. This has helped to offset the decline in revenues from diminished oil prices. From the point of view of the United States it should be noted that during the period of reforms there occurred increases "of approximately 48% in imports of intermediate and capital goods, and more than 150% in imports of consumer goods" (Inter-American Development Bank 1989: 381). At the same time, by 1988 Mexico had displaced West Germany as the United States' third trading partner, next only to Canada and Japan showing an annual 25% increase in its purchases from the north in 1988 after liberalization. By 1989, Senator Bill Bradley (D-NJ) was able to write of the new image of Mexico:

They have reduced their internal budget deficit by the equivalent of nearly 3 Gramm-Rudmans. They have cut their trade barriers by two-thirds. They have sold off massive quantities of the public enterprises. They have joined GATT. They have allowed 100 percent foreign ownership by regulation, and

Figure 2.2   US-Mexican Bilateral Trade ($ Millions)

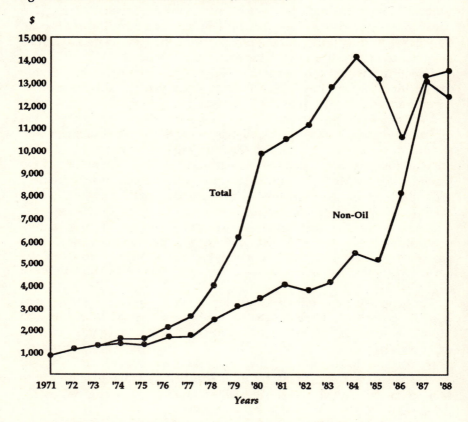

Source: Comercio Exterior: Banco Nacional de Comercio Exterior, SNC

will probably do so by statute. So they have squeezed their economy, but gotten no growth dividend (Bradley 1989a).

These changes are no simple process of economic adjustment; they require a realistic appreciation on the part of the United States of the political climate within which they have to be effected. Writing in 1986 Castenada foretold the difficulties—difficulties which have been faced by the last two administrations in Mexico:

All of these reforms, then, have the same drawbacks: they are politically costly, economically destabilizing in the short run, require long lead times, and would tarnish the government's nationalistic progressive image. The

Mexican political system is accustomed to implementing exactly the opposite type of change: politically expedient, economically painless, profitable in the short run, and in accordance with the government's traditional rhetoric (Castenada 1986: 299).

Presidential candidate Cuauhtemoc Cardenas, writing in the New York Times in 1990, pointed out that the economic reforms had far outrun, and threatened to substitute for, real political change:

The decision by Mexico's president . . . to consider a free trade area with the US should not divert attention from the salient problem facing Mexico; the status of the Institutional Revolutionary Party as one of the last remaining authoritarian political systems in the world. . . . The government hopes to manage the dilemma of separating the political and economic reform by relying on US financing and on Washington's political support. The regime is gambling that it can buy off the country's middle classes and neutralize popular discontent with the help of American resources, thus containing demands for democratization . . . . The true debate lies in who should pay the unavoidable costs of restructuring. To date, the Mexican workers—through sharply lower real wages and dramatic cuts in education, health and housing expenditures—have carried a disproportionate share of the burden (Cardenas 1990).

For these reasons the government has kept in place tight control over prices, and has backtracked on the original program of debt-equity arrangements. Wages have fallen in real terms (the 1986 level only 57% of what it was in real terms a decade before), and the rise in the price of staple goods has been a source of continuing concern. But, we must never lose sight of the impressive scale and scope of what has already been achieved, and the need for the reforms to receive sympathetic and cooperative understanding by trade partners. There is a strong need to counter rising protectionist sentiment in the United States with regard to the "threat" from a growing Mexican industrial sector. The growth is likely to be in areas already under stress in the United States economy such as textiles, automobile assembly, shoes, etc. Other countries have coped with this sort of change by moving to the higher-quality end of the market or through structural shifts, but, in writing about the *maquiladora* industries in 1989, the *Christian Science Monitor* noted: "[US] union officials, industry executives, and some congressmen from 'rust-belt' states have argued that [they] steal American jobs, threaten the electronics industry [referring to Japanese enterprises there], and may be designed to circumvent United States trade laws" (*Christian Science Monitor* August 8, 1989). The alarm of organized labor, which is already mobilizing to resist any suggestion of a free trade area, arises from the fact that wages in Mexico are about one-eighth of those in the United States, leading to a potential relocation of industry. Industrialists have pointed out that, of every $1 of economic growth in Mexico, approximately 15¢ is spent in the United States.

The Foreign Relations Climate

Traditionally the US relationship with Mexico has demonstrated the former country's view of the latter as one of the turbulent countries of the southern cone, in contrast to the way it has viewed Canada. Such characterizations have been encapsulated in foreign policy pronouncements since the time of Monroe, followed by Theodore Roosevelt and Taft. Under Franklin Roosevelt's "good neighbor" policy the climate matured somewhat, but Mexico's perception of its northern neighbor is still a living embodiment of a history which included 14 invasions and four occupations, and at best, a paternalistic stance or indifference.

During the last decade relations with Mexico worsened over a series of issues including drugs, illegal immigration, the debt issue, and the United States' Central America policy. In fact, very often the portrayal of Mexico's role in many of these issues was a serious distortion of reality, ignoring, for example, Mexico's active pursuit of those in the drug trade, its desire to create growth and jobs at home, and its adherence to the non-intervention clause of the OAS Charter. But the perception of Mexico held by the United States was another matter. Increasingly the whole "Mexican business" was perceived by United States politicians as aspects of the "border issue."

Reality and perception are often at odds in this story. The reality is that the Mexican border is one of the longest, and certainly the most frequently crossed, in the world, and has for the last 70 or so years been remarkably open and trouble free. The fact that Mexico and the United States agree only about 14% of the time when voting at the United Nations is not a reflection of outright hostility and opposition, but of the very different perspective of hemispheric affairs and the role of the United States as seen from Mexico. Tensions are bound to arise where power is so asymmetrically distributed and where the cultural background and global affiliations are so different. Mexico is clearly a leader among non-aligned developing countries and its global stance is based solidly on principle. The United States is a global superpower and its stance is often based on ideological standoffs, a longstanding sense of exceptionalism, and strategic power plays. In such a climate the potential for nervousness on Mexico's part is not unlikely. As one writer put it succinctly: "Mexico's foreign policy is captive to an historically based psychological need to assert a sense of nationalistic independence vis-á-vis the United States. A morbid fear of losing both national identity and sovereignty compels the Mexican nation state to continually define itself in terms of its distance from the United States" (Delal Baer 1983: 107).

While it is unlikely that generations of suspicion can be swept away overnight, there is a growing sense of a changed context and new possibilities. Even in the diminishing climate of Cold War confrontation, it is still important to the United States that its southern neighbor be a stable one with a healthy environment—which can then hold its own population in situ:

> Mexico's proximity to the US will continue to prove of great value to its [Mexico's] development—not because illegal immigrants can cross the border, thereby relieving pressure on the Mexican economy, but because the US cannot tolerate an unstable country on its border. To preclude such a development the US will continue to encourage trade and investment in Mexico and to support international loans and agreements and industrial development credits for Mexico (Gilbreath 1986: 14).

In fact, the intervention of the US presidency in putting pressure on Mexico's creditors to ease the burden and allow breathing space for reform is evidence of the US concern at the executive level.

The confrontational picture of the 1980s has been replaced, toward the end of the decade, by one of more convergent views. The coming to power, first of de la Madrid, and more particularly, Salinas, has put in place a cabinet with a strong North American perspective based on their familiarity with, or higher education in, the United States. This by no means makes them creatures of the United States, but it allows for a more successful bridging of the perception gap between the two countries. The foreign policy picture of the 1990s is a very different one from even a generation ago. Now the range of actors is very much greater: businessmen, federal agencies, commercial banks, tourists, the immigration services, and a rapidly increasing number of one country's residents domiciled in the other country (there are 50,000 US citizens in Baha California alone). But it is Mexico's rapid growth of trade, and its increasingly sophisticated and less "Third World" nature, which promote a new foreign relations climate. Representative Kolbe (R-AZ) said in 1988:

> Economic events drove the two countries closer together. For the US, it was a mounting trade deficit and the challenge of international competitiveness. For Mexico, it was the need to diversify after the collapse of the oil market. These translated into extraordinary initiatives by both administrations to reach out to each other—their willingness for example, to negotiate the US-Mexico Framework Agreement of 1987 (Kolbe 1988: 14).

For years the United States has manifested a *modus vivendi* with Mexico's foreign policy, thereby accepting Mexico's need to stand by its principles and affiliation with the developing world. This was severely tested during the Reagan era, but has improved under Bush. However, building bridges with the United States in the context of the action in Panama has been made extremely difficult domestically for the reformist government in Mexico City because the invasion tends to reemphasize the old imbalance of power, the suspicion of US hegemony in the hemisphere, as well as awakening memories of General Pershing, the Marines in Vera Cruz, and other events still in most Mexicans' memories of yesterday.

Toward a Common Economic Union

There is an old Chinese curse which states: "May all your dreams come true." The phenomenal success of recent trade liberalization policies in Mexico have the potential to exact retaliation from the United States; a retaliation which might be most effectively avoided by the creation of a free trade area between the two states. The extremely high degree of economic interdependence between the two countries is a reality, as the Bilateral Commission noted: "Indeed, the Commission has not been able to think of another pair of countries—including the United States and Canada—whose interrelationship is as penetrating as that of Mexico and the United States" (Bilateral Commission 1989: 144). Exports to the United States have risen from 55% of the total in 1982 to more than 70% today. Writing in 1984 Weintraub noted even then that: ". . . . the trade and financial interconnections that already exist make independent Mexican macroeconomic policies infeasible in any event" (Weintraub 1984: 172). There are two possible problems with the simple continuation of present liberalization policies. In the first instance (the Chinese curse), the sheer success of Mexico's export-led industrialization invites retaliation within a purely bilateral arrangement:

> Moreover, as Mexico's export capacity expands, it is likely that a larger set of [US] import restrictions will become binding, and that new ones will be implemented. [Footnote] The fact that two-thirds of United States' countervailing duties investigations instigated against Mexican products involved products with a previous export increase of more than 50 percent illustrates the likelihood of this event (Trigueros 1989: 265).

The second point concerns how feasible it is to go much further with the present liberalization arrangements. Trigueros thinks that "the possibility of further trade liberalization is now practically absent," and the way forward involves a change in the nature of the trading, or even economic, relationship between the two states. The alternative would seem to be a rapid growth in areas of economic competition and conflict (Smith 1989: 10), and so this is a very critical time in establishing the future direction. The Framework Agreement between the two countries has offered some opportunity for conflict resolution and accord on problem avoidance, but it might appear that it is hardly possible at this point to talk about a shared vision, especially in light of the recent Trade Act and the protectionist lobby in the United States. "Without a positive, shared vision of the future, bilateral economic relations will increasingly become occasions for conflict instead of cooperation and growth" (Bilateral Commission 1989: 73). There is certainly no question of Mexico redirecting its export-led industrialization back into the protectionist mold, even though it might be pointed out that this is what Korea did. Korea, however, did not start out with a base of existing, uncompetitive industries.

Furthermore, the high degree of connectivity in trade between the United States and Mexico is unlikely to change significantly. Even though Mexico was pursuing a diversification strategy, alternative investors and consumers, such as Japan, individually form a tiny proportion of the market. When Canada pursued a similar diversification program it did hardly anything to change the established trade pattern to the south (Weintraub 1984: 174). This sense of the "inevitable" may well have been a major factor in the ultimately successful passage of the Canadian Free Trade legislation. A visit by President Salinas to Europe in January 1990 appears to have alarmed him very considerably. At that time he came away with a sense of the real preoccupation with eastern Europe, and the virtual neglect and indifference surrounding the Mexican success story. In contrast to the rush to create new funds for recovery in former communist states, Mexico continued totally outside the US aid circuit. After this visit things began to move rapidly. The establishment of a legislated framework of guaranteed access to the United States, at truly competitive terms, would provide Mexico with the climate of confidence necessary to keep its momentum going. There certainly has been no evidence of the threatened results of liberalization so far: mass closures of uneconomic establishments or a consumer market swamped with cheap imports. Indeed the growth in the economy is overwhelmingly stimulated by exports rather than by any changes in aggregate domestic demand, and so the climate for maintaining exports, which *de facto* means to the United States, is essential.

Recent writings (Weintraub, Bilateral Commission, Trigueros, *inter alia*), stress the need to move the bilateral relationship onto a more comprehensive, free trade basis. This is nothing new. When Ronald Reagan was running for president the first time, in the speech announcing his candidacy he devoted a quarter of the time to US relations with Canada and Mexico:

> Before his first election Reagan pushed the idea of a North American Common Market based on his experience as governor of California. In 1981 his administration told him that it was not feasible. Memories of the past make many Mexicans wary of the special relationship with the United States (Purcell 1981: 383).

Subsequently Mr. Bush, with his Texas background, advocated a free trade area during his campaign for the presidency: "As president," he promised, "I will work toward the creation of a free trade zone embracing Mexico, Canada and the United States." He subsequently appointed two like-minded, Texan supporters as Secretary of State (Baker), and Secretary of Commerce (Mossbacher). Texans are sensitive to the opportunities offered by free trade as compensation for declining military and oil revenues in this border state.

There was also a suspicion, so close to the second oil-price shock, that this was a ploy to secure freer access to Mexican oil. Lopez-Portillo and Pierre Trudeau of Canada issued a statement in 1980 saying that "current informal proposals for trilateral economic cooperation among Canada, the United States and Mexico . . . would not serve the best interests of the country" (Weintraub 1984: 183). Initially, also, Mr. Salinas stated in January 1988, just after his appointment: "I am not in favor of any free trade or common market plan because there is such a different economic level between the United States and Mexico." This reluctance was to change dramatically after his 1990 European visit.

Reagan took up the call again in 1988 during a meeting with de la Madrid in Mazatlan, though reservations were expressed again by the Mexicans and some members of the US Congress. However, the dramatic change in the relationship with Canada left some Mexicans feeling they were in danger of being left behind, especially as Canada had previously expressed many of the same reservations as were still being expressed in Mexico. This time in Congress there was some strong talk in favor of extending the free-trade area to include Mexico. Writing about a House Concurrent Resolution that he introduced, Senator Kolbe (R-AZ) stated:

> An FTA will help both countries sell more goods and services to each other and enable them to bring their combined productive resources to bear against economic competition from southeast Asia and the European Community. An FTA could help Mexico with its foreign debt. It could ease the US trade deficit . . . . Taken together with the US-Canada accord—which will eliminate most major trade barriers by 1999—a US-Mexico FTA will be one step closer toward the North American Common Market that must exist to compete in the twentieth century (Kolbe 1988: 15).

The global trading climate is an important factor bearing on the need for urgent consideration of a FTA by Mexico. The 1980s represented a period of increasingly managed trade, giving rise to some alarm in the United States. The prospect of the emergence of "fortress Europe" in 1992 is seen by some as diminishing the ability of the United States to sell in that market. Although the US administration has pursued freer trade through the Uruguay Round of talks, concern is expressed in such statements as that by

Senator Bill Bradley when he said, addressing the Commonwealth Club in San Francisco ". . . it makes sense for the US to pursue other efforts at economic coordination while the European Community works out its new rules" (Bradley 1989B: quoted in the *Christian Science Monitor*, March 29). Bradley had been referring to a Pacific "coalition" of eight countries (including Mexico). However, there has also been open discussion of the possibility of a Free Trade Area with Japan (*Far East Economic Review* 13, October 1988: 85), first raised by Mike Mansfield during his tenure as US ambassador to Tokyo (Barlas 1988: 2). The suggestion was given greater visibility when Japanese premier Noburu Takeshita visited Washington in 1988: "he responded favorably to a suggestion from the then-Senate majority leader Robert Byrd (D-W.Va.) that America and Japan join in a free-trade pact" (Whenmouth 1988: 61). There was concern in Washington, however, when Australia called a conference in November 1989 to discuss closer economic cooperation among 11 countries with Pacific interests. Initially the United States was not invited. Commenting on the meeting, the *Economist* noted: " [as exchange rate management advances in East Asia] Japan will begin to play the sort of role in Asia that West Germany already does in Western Europe. The result is that, unlike the European Community, which began life as a customs union that would eventually move on to monetary matters, Asia could begin the other way round" (*Economist*, 1989a). This prospect is very unsettling for the United States, that the US could become isolated between two great blocs, or try to rush into a FTA merger with one of them (Smith, 1988: 85). In Mexico this raises fears of a "northern alliance" that could isolate the south and deflect resources (Smith 1989: 13).

An entire paper this length could be written on the implications of Mexico's $100 billion foreign debt, but here we limit our observations to the debt for closer economic union. Since most of the debt was incurred for largely non-productive purposes it mortgaged the future of Mexico to a return of higher oil prices which never arrived. The need to meet interest payments, even under rescheduling arrangements spurred the diversification of the economy into liberalization and export-led manufacturing growth, with the encouragement of the IMF. However, with one-third of government expenditure going to meet interest payments on the debt, the public sector is hard pressed to provide the infrastructure improvements necessary for a modern economy, while the uncertainty engendered by the situation acts as a deterrent to foreign investors. The major debt agreements of November 1989 and February 1990 have, at least, stabilized the situation, and removed much of the uncertainty, so that foreign reserves have reached record highs. A FTA would allow Mexico to sustain its remarkable growth and move to a situation where greater manufacturing growth in the country as a whole, rather than just in the *maquiladora* belt, would permit a much larger proportion of the earnings to be retained at home. This, in turn, would permit the country to put the fears of the debt situation behind it, and have a longer-term vision. While the restoration of confidence and expectations would, possibly, reopen the commercial lending market for development capital, rather than just the meeting of interest payments which has dominated up to now.

By becoming part of a Free Trade Area with the United States, Mexico would be locked into a system that would eliminate most of the threats of being closed out of a northern club. Instead it could become a founding member of such an organization. Without this institutional guarantee there is likely to be a problem arising from the fact that most of the growth in the US economy, and that of Mexico, arises from export promotion. This contains the seeds of bitter conflict and rivalry without the "shared vision" mentioned above. Canada has already expressed its sympathy for the expansion of the Area, having stated: "Canada is not opposed to a third party joining. However, it should be understood that an agreement reached with the United States should be open to accession, subsequently, by third parties, just as the European Common Market provided for expansion (Canadian Senate Standing Committee on Foreign Affairs 1980: vol. 2. 123). Free Trade Areas are not outside the terms of GATT, and are seen by some in the United States as providing additional leverage for the expansion of freer trade at the Uruguay Round discussions (Weintraub 1984: 185). Barlas noted: "The bilateral agreements send a message to GATT—as does the . . . Trade Bill which targets retaliation at those who are not dealing fairly with the United States" (Barlas 1988: 2).

Within the European Community there have been major econometric studies on the costs and benefits of the system, such as the study on the "costs of non-Europe." There have been no such detailed quantitative studies for a Mexico-United States community, but the consensus is strongly in favor of moving, at least, to the freeing of trade, or the creation of a Free Trade Area. Kreinin summarized the benefits as follows:

> Economic efficiency in Mexico would benefit from a FTA on both sides of the trade equation. Increased imports would add competitive pressure on Mexican industry, forcing reorganization, rationalization and the reallocation of resources. Freer access to export markets would enable Mexico to move toward greater specialization in products in which it possesses a comparative advantage. Since Mexico's advantage is in labor-intensive industries, this specialization should increase demand for labor, reduce disguised unemployment, increase earnings, and lessen the pressure to emigrate north of the border. Longer production runs and economies of scale in production and distribution would follow. Finally, the nonreversible removal of protection would spur both foreign and domestic investment (Kreinin 1981: 30).

The existence of the FTA would also help remove the penalties of progressive tariff rates now in existence relating to the degree of value-added on exports, thus helping to free Mexico from the Third World pattern of trade. Kreinin went on to outline three factors that emphasized the attraction of a FTA between the two countries. He stated that: (i) the greater the size of the integrating area, the greater the likelihood of trade creation. Furthermore, the greater the share of intra-area trade in the country's total trade prior to integration, the greater the scope for trade creation (more than 70% in Mexico's case); (ii) the less similar the type of products produced by the two countries, the less likely they are to displace each other; and (iii) the larger the size of the production cost differentials between the countries in each of the various industries, so the larger the differential, the greater the scope for trade displacement [from outside]. For all three of these he says that "one can expect a large trade creation in the case of North American integration" (Kreinin 1981: 13).

Anticipating some hostility from interest groups representing beleaguered industries in the United States, and from the protectionist lobby in general, Weintraub estimated:

> The case for free trade from the US standpoint would not rest on increasing US exports by diverting the exports of others, but rather by the dynamic effects this would have on Mexico. This would, in turn, stimulate US dynamism, thereby augmenting both US and third-country exports. The USinterest in bilateral free trade thus rests on a combination of efficiency and industry dynamism. In these respects, the US objectives would be the same as those of Mexico (Weintraub 1984: 179).

Of course the movement toward closer economic union in North America is not just an economic question for Mexico. The ruling Institutional Revolutionary Party is already under pressure at home from the rise of opposition parties, now gaining seats for the first time in PRI history. Clearly, Mexico is not Canada, and the problems of integration into a trade community would be potentially much more disruptive, since the country's economy is both traditionally more protected, and more underdeveloped. There would be no real possibility of total reciprocity in the short run, and there would be a need for a realistic period of transition to allow for Mexico to adjust. But this is established practice in the European Community where countries as different as Portugal and the German Federal Republic have to be accommodated. The shock effect on Mexico's wages, prices, inflation and monetary situation would be alarming if the impact of the Economic Solidarity Pact were suddenly to be removed. There is no doubt also, that an FTA represents a limited loss of sovereignty, but for the authorities in Mexico there is a need to find a balance between historical nervousness about their northern neighbor, and finding a means to provide the growth to generate jobs, win favor, and prevent the strengthening of the opposition in the short run. At the same time: "many observers see increasing signs of a slow awakening in certain northern communities of a dormant streak in

Mexican consciousness favoring closer links with the United States. . . . [The] PAN [party] is more pro-US, and is increasingly favored by the disenchanted middle class" (Castenada 1986: 291). So the government is under pressure from many directions on this issue. However, without the income from export-led growth, which means to the United States, there is unlikely to be any basis for winning support on any side. The Mexican economy could not support a slide back into protectionism. The Bilateral Commission's opinion was that the

> trade agreement between the United States and Canada is [not] a suitable framework for trade relations between the United States and Mexico. Unlike Canada, Mexico could not be expected to eliminate all tariffs and export subsidies quickly. More importantly, Mexico is unlikely soon to bind itself to eliminate the differences in domestic and export energy prices, agree to national treatment for foreign investment services, or totally foreswear safeguards, investment-related performance requirements, and the use of government procurement as a development instrument (Bilateral Commission 1989: 64-65).

What this tends to overlook is (i) the need for the "shared vision" to counter protectionism and the rise of blocs; (ii) the fact that all these issues had to be faced—or remain to be faced—in the European Community; and (iii) the remarkable degree to which change has already occurred with spectacular results that need to be preserved and encouraged. It is not so long ago, after all, that Kreinin was writing that formal integration between Canada and the United States was an idea whose time had not come since: "even in Canada there is a widespread fear that with integration Canadians will become hewers of wood and drawers of water" (Kreinin 1981: 7). It is undeniable that there are many problems concerning the loss of sovereignty, limitations on policy instruments at home, and short-term dislocations (Mrs. Thatcher has outlined them repeatedly), however, setting a target of a FTA does not mean that everything must happen at once. It gives, like 1992, a target that, as Dr. Johnson said "concentrates the mind wonderfully."

Where Next?

We have learned from Europe 1992, the sudden arrival of the Canadian-US Free Trade Agreement, and events in Eastern Europe, that the established mores of today's history may not have much predictive impact. As Kennedy (1988), has shown, the old-established order of great power economics has been transformed into a very fluid multi-polar world in which readjustment is the order of the day and ancient rivalries can be put into what Trotsky called the "dustbin of history."

Once regional free trade is established, then this may well create the foundation for further advances. This has been the pattern in the European Community where it has become increasingly difficult to distinguish between what is economic and what is political. In the case of Mexico, Canada, and the United States, the present level of debate is, of course, restricted purely to trade. But as the economies develop within the context of the freer movement of goods, there will be greater and greater pressures for the free movement of capital and labor. If Mexico's growth is sustained and enhanced through free trade, then there may be less reason for anyone in the United States to fear the eventual unrestricted movement of labor. Certainly the growth potential of Mexico with a greatly expanded market for its goods would require huge injections of capital which, at present, the underdeveloped domestic capital market—despite high Mexican savings levels—is unable to meet. This free flow of capital would, in turn, create jobs to hold more people at home and improve the domestic market: "it has become apparent that trade barriers tend to exacerbate migration" (Reynolds and McCleery 1985: 217). All of this accords well with US ambitions for Mexico. In the short run it raises fears of loss of sovereignty in Mexico, and foreign domination of sensitive areas of the economy. It also raises questions about a fundamental shift of affiliation, for Mexico is traditionally allied with the Latin countries, and its standing among them might be compromised by what could be seen as a sell-out to the "north." On the other hand, Mexico's standing among its peers is more likely to be influenced by its economic health and strength, than by its voting alliances at the United Nations. Attempts by Mexico to achieve free trade benefits with its southern neighbors (LAFTA, LAIA, CACM, etc.) all ended in failure because they were essentially trying to sell the same things to other small, relatively poor economies. Mexico is skeptical about going any further along that road, it is unlikely to retreat into protectionism; and it is now in a position where more, rather than less, economic attachment to the United States seems inevitable.

If the Mexican economy continues to perform as it has after 1986, and if—as now seems more likely—the benefits are not totally gobbled up by the debt overhang, then there will emerge ever more need for closer capital and labor arrangements with the United States. The latter, feeling more secure that everyone in Mexico is not planning to escape from an absence of opportunity, will be more inclined to treat the need it has for labor from Mexico on a positive and more open basis. One study has calculated that opening the labor market between the two countries on an immediate basis would produce an estimated eight million migrants in the first year, which would be unacceptable. However, the same study states that:

There is an identifiable tradeoff between United States investment in Mexico and migration to this country. In our model an annual flow of $5 billion would reduce the stock of migrants to this country by 200,000 per year on a cumulative basis....The stock of Mexican migrants in the United States peaks at 3.5 million (1.5 million below the status quo peak of 5 million in 1995)....By the year 2000 this scenario leads to a ... return flow of migrants (Reynolds and McCleery 1985: 221).

Some might criticize this review of the Mexican situation for its lack of econometric exactitude. The fact is that the decisions that have to be made will be almost entirely political, or if economic, in terms of broad sweeps of the inevitable, rather than fine tuning the options. Econometric studies are more likely to be used to justify, or modify, political initiatives than to generate them. Briefly: Mexico is overwhelmingly locked into the US economy, and there is no real alternative: this is Mexico's only realistic option for creating growth and stability at home. The climate of protectionism abroad and the rise of trading blocs makes it imperative that Mexico consolidate its position with the United States as quickly as possible, and that the accommodation should be one that provides an overall and lasting context for the freeing of trade—and later, capital, and labor. A North American free trade area would, after all, have a per capita GNP 7.7% higher than that of the European Community, and a consumer base of 350 million people. There can be, and will have to be, a long and sympathetic transition period. Compromises will have to be made. Europe's economic community developed through constant compromise as did the United States. But the "shared vision," a 1992 for Mexico, must be there. There really is no viable, lasting alternative.

Toward an Economic Community

If the past is any predictor of the future we would expect to see, in the relatively near future, a free trade agreement between the United States and Mexico. Because of the very different circumstances characterizing the Canadian and Mexican economies, it would be unlikely that this agreement would be the same as the Canadian-US FTA. Indeed, the Bilateral Commission made it clear that the Canadian model would not serve for Mexico. The later country has a much greater task of disengaging itself from a much more highly-protected industrial heritage. Thus, in the short run, there would have to be fairly substantial concessions within a transition phase. Indeed, during the months immediately preceding the ratification of the Canadian-US FTA, there were talks between the three countries to include Mexico in the FTA (Srodes 1988: 16). Because Mexican issues would have required several more months of negotiation and pressures were building to come to closure to ratify the Canadian-US FTA, however, a tripartite Canadian-Mexican-US FTA was not realized. At the moment Canadian exports to Mexico form only about 1% of total Canadian exports, while for Mexico the figure is around 5%.

Even with such an FTA or two FTAs in place, that would not create a North American Economic Community. It would however, establish the "shared vision" mentioned above. Providing the agreements do not go badly wrong either politically or economically in the short run, and providing the dispute mechanisms prove adequate to the job in hand, then the natural question will be "what next?"

An FTA is not an economic community since it normally does not include provision for the free movement of labor or capital, neither does it have any shared economic or social policy, except by coincidence. There will still be major national differences on such issues as common industrial regulations standards. Some provisions of the Canadian-US FTA lay the groundwork for future liberalization of trade and harmonization of regulations, and thus may help the process of translating a shared vision into reality. For example, Canada and the United States agreed to continue negotiations over five to seven years to develop a new set of rules governing domestic subsidies and countervailing duties involving trade in lumber and uranium. Also, the FTA moved well beyond existing provisions of the GATT in the areas of government procurement, dispute settlement procedure under the GATT is badly in need of improvement, and the threshold amounts are much higher in the GATT ($171,000 versus $25,000 in the FTA). In four service sectors, architecture, tourism, computer and telecommunications-network services, detailed annexes of the FTA provide for the reduction of non-tariff barriers and the development of common regulatory standards. The dispute settlement mechanisms of the FTA establish important principles: in cases involving countervailing duties, the consistency of final orders with national laws and GATT obligations will be subject to binding arbitration. In other, general cases, the FTA creates early-warning consultations to preempt disputes, more expeditious procedures, and decisionmaking by binational panels that should lead to a convergence in national trade laws (Horlick, Oliver, and Steger 1988: 65-86).

The 1985 Mexico-US agreement on subsidies and countervailing duties, while not as far-reaching as similar provisions in the Canada-US FTA, is a step toward free trade. The 1985 agreement served as "a surrogate for Mexican accession to the GATT subsidies code," and it "helped defuse a number of bilateral subsidy/countervail disputes by imposing disciple on Mexican subsidy programs and by requiring an injury test in US countervail cases affecting Mexican goods" (Schott 1989: 43). There are striking parallels between Canadian and Mexican concerns over the US countervailing duty law, on the one hand, and US concerns about domestic subsidies in Canada and Mexico, on the other. There is little doubt that Mexico would welcome the same sort of agreement the United States made with Canada to prior consultation on prospective changes in the US countervailing duty law and to binding arbitration in such cases. However, the failure of US negotiations to reach any agreement with the Canadians on a set of rules governing subsidies and the subsequent negative reaction in Congress cast serious doubt on a Mexico-US accord that is not balanced with subsidies rules.

In the case of Mexico it can be argued that a similar FTA is the natural next step. As we have seen, Mexico requires a very considerable amount of investment to continue to drive the export-led growth. The past record, and the international capacity of the economy to provide these funds, even with Mexico's relatively high savings rate, is inadequate to the task. Given sufficient confidence at home and abroad in the Mexican economy, the country might be prepared to reduce restrictions on US and Canadian investments. Concern has already been expressed in the Canadian press regarding the movement of Canadian industry, not to the United States, but to the Mexican *maquiladora*. The major recent renegotiations of the debt situation improve this climate of confidence. In the short run this freer movement of capital could be restricted to certain sectors of the economy which require private investment on a scale unlikely to be realized at home. Here, too, there can be provision for a transition period. None of these recommendations mean that every thing has to be done overnight. There will have to be a political and economic compromise to prevent the Mexican population from feeling that they are having their country bought from under their feet, somewhat akin to sentiment in some areas of the United States about the Japanese. Realistic joint ventures can be encouraged, but the across-the-board 51% Mexican participation requirement has proved a deterrent to serious investors from outside.

As we have seen, Canadians have similar fears about the domination of US investors, and the Canadian-US FTA makes only very modest inroads on Canadian restrictions against foreign (i.e., US) investment. The difference, of course, is that US and other foreign capital have flowed into Canada in substantial measure to contribute to economic development, with the result that Canada has the ninth highest GNP in the world (compared to Mexico at fourteenth place). The FTA will undoubtedly cause some of the more protected Canadian (and US) industries to enlarge and modernize if they are to survive, as, indeed, Mexican industries would have to under free trade with the United States. However, the overall long-term effect of the FTA, most analysts agree, will be economic expansion as firms increase investment to supply the larger market.

It is only the continued expansion of the Mexican economy which can provide the confidence and opportunity to bring back money from outside. The old belief that anything other than the strictest exchange controls would lead to a flood of money out of the country is totally wrong. The money went anyway, and the only thing that encourages it to stay at home is the prospect of a reasonable return on capital without the fear of runaway inflation, devaluation, and the wiping out of savings. Given these conditions, the money will both stay and return. Major foreign investments in Mexico will, in turn, stimulate a demand for goods and services of a type produced at home.

Recent foreign and domestic investment in manufacturing has led to the doubling of exports of manufactured goods from 1985 to 1989, as we have seen. With over two-thirds of these exports going to the United States, with whom Mexico has been running very sizeable trade surpluses, it is to be expected that Mexico shares Canada's strong interest in developing assurances that they will not be shut out by US protectionist tendencies. As Mexico struggles to modernize, under the heavy burden of its foreign debt, it understands very clearly the advantages of a free trade agreement now, and an economic community later, as insurance against a fortress America. Lastly, it seems that only *sustained* export-led growth in Mexico is going to provide for the countervailing opportunity necessary to provide some reduction in the push and pull factors of migration. A popular vision might be that the moment there is any provision for the free movement of labor, then Mexico will become another East Germany. But, just as in East Germany, the answer may well be to create closer economic union (though we are not suggesting a unification of Mexico and the United States!) It is hard to see how anything but the closer integration of the two economies will deal with the problem of "illegals." In terms of the intimate economic links that have developed over the last decade between Mexico and the United States, and the tremendous vulnerability of the former to bilateral adjustments such as protectionism, the expansion of common policy into economic alignment, labor and capital concessions seems almost inevitable.

US Foreign Policy and a North American Community

We are, as another Chinese proverb has it, "living in interesting times." Many of the old ground rules, territorial divisions, rules of sovereignty, and other well-established contexts of foreign policy management, have undergone radical change. In this very fluid environment the United States has at least four cards on the table in terms of its position vis-á-vis international trade. These may be summarized as:

1. If the world is rapidly moving into major regional trading blocs, then the United States should get in on the ground floor rather as the Japanese have done in the United States, and make a major move to secure on-site US investment in Europe before the "fortress" is finally established—if it ever is. Hence the encouragement of greater US investment in the EEC.

2. If, again, blocs are to be the order of the day, then the US should not waste any time before creating its own expanding regional trade environment. Hence the prospect of a North American Community.

3. Whatever is happening in terms of regional groupings, the United States should pursue its traditional post-war policy of pressing for ever-greater openness in world trade. Hence the attitude of the US in the current Uruguay Round of talks at GATT.

4. Whatever is going on in the rest of the world looks like bad news, and the openness of the United States' market is simply being exploited by a lot of tricky players on an uneven field. The best approach then is "damn the torpedoes" and let the country look inward for its salvation with protectionism winning the day.

Such an array of seemingly conflicting policy options is confusing for those inside and outside the US system. However, it is not as contradictory as it sometimes looks. The thrust toward freer trade within GATT is a continuing one, and there is nothing in GATT which restricts the development of a North American Free Trade Area, unless its external tariff becomes, on average, higher than the cumulative situation of what went before, and no-one has suggested that, though Mexico would have a hard time surviving US levels of external tariff in the short run. At the same time, some have argued in speeches quoted in this paper, that a NAFTA or NAC would greatly strengthen the stand of the United States in bargaining for freer trade. Finally, it makes good political sense to some on the Hill to have a solid fall-back position if the country's worst fears about the intentions of their trade partners and trade rivals come true. So, it is not possible to say exactly where, in foreign policy terms, the creation of a FTA is leading. It would have a part to play in several options, and there is no reason, as the Canadian Senate has said, why this should be an end in itself: it could expand south or west. That is truly star-gazing. But the events of the last decade may very well be interpreted as laying the foundations for a North American arena of economic activity.

References

Barlas, S. (1989). "Trading blocs may block world trade." *Marketing News*. 10, 10. 2 and 23.

Bilateral Commission on the Future of United States-Mexican Relations (1989). *The challenge of interdependence*. University Press of America. Lanham MD. 238pp.

Bradley, W. (1989a). "Mexico. A debt test case." *Christian Science Monitor*. July 19. (1989).

————. (1989b) Speech to the Commonwealth Club/World Affairs Council. San Francisco. March 29.

Brown, D. K. and Stern, R. M. (1987). "A Modelling Perspective." In Stern, R. M., Trezise, P.H. and Whalley, J. (eds.), *Perspectives on a US-Canadian Free Trade Agreement*. The Brookings Institution.

Cardenas, C. (1990). "For Mexico, freedom before free trade." *New York Times*. April 1990.

Castenada, J. G. (1986). "Mexico at the brink." *Foreign Affairs*. 64. 287-303.

Crandall, R. W. (1987). "A Sectoral Perspective: Steel." In Stern, R. M., Trezise, P.H. and Whalley, J. (eds.), *Perspectives on a US-Canadian Free Trade Agreement*. The Brookings Institution.

d'Aquino, T. (1988). "The Canada-United States Free Trade Agreement: Myth and Reality." *Vital Speeches*. 55. 54-58.

Delal Baer, M. (1987). "Mexico. Ambivalent ally." *Washington Quarterly*. 10, 3. Summer. 103-113.

Economist. (1988). "Canada Survey." October 8. 1-18.

———. (1989a). "Puffery in the Pacific." November 11. 15.

———. (1989b). "America and Mexico. Happy times." October 7. 27-28.

Gilbreath, K. (1986). "A businessman's guide to the Mexican economy." *Columbia Journal of World Business*. Summer. 3-14.

Hamilton, B. and Whalley, J. (1985). "Geographically Discriminatory Trade Arrangements." *Review of Economics and Statistics*. 67. August. 446-455.

Harris, R. G. (1985). "Summary of a Project on the General Equilibrium Evaluation of Canadian Trade Policy." In Hill, R. and Whalley, J. (eds.), *Canada-United States Free Trade*. University of Toronto Press.

Harris, R. and Cox, D. (1985). "Trade Liberalization and Industrial Organization: Some Estimates for Canada." *Journal of Political Economy*. 93. February. 115-145.

Hill, R. and Whalley, J. (1985). "Canada-US Free Trade: An Introduction." In Whalley, J. and Hill, R. (eds.), *Canada-US Free Trade*. University of Toronto Press. 1-12.

Horlick, G. N., Oliver, G. D., and Steger, D. P. (1988). "Dispute Resolution Mechanisms." In Schott, J. J. and Smith, M. G. (eds.), *The Canada-United States Free Trade Agreement: The Global Impact*. Institute for International Economics. 65-86.

Hufbauer, G. C. and Samet, A. J. (1985). "US Response to Canadian Initiatives for Sectoral Trade Liberalization: 1983-84." In Stairs, D. and Winham, G. R. (eds.), *The Politics of Canada's Economic Relationship with the United States*. University of Toronto Press.

Inter-American Development Bank (1989). *Economic and social progress in Latin America*.

Kennedy, Paul. (1987). *The Rise and Fall of the Great Powers*. Random House.

Kolbe, J. (1988). "US-Mexico relations: Building a golden age." *Economic Development Review*. 6, 3. 14-17.

Kreinin, M. E. (1981). "North American economic integration." *Law and Contemporary Problems*. 44. Summer. 7-31.

Lecuona, R. A. (1988). "A North American common market: An idea whose time has come?" In Fatemi, A. *International trade and finance—A North American perspective*. Praeger. 259-269.

Little, J. S. (1988). "At Stake in the US-Canada Free Trade Agreement: Modest Gains or a Significant Setback?" *New England Economic Review*. May/June. 3-20.

Luis Rubio, F. (1987). "Economic structure of Mexico." *California Western International Law Journal*. 18. 13-20.

MacDonald Royal Commission on the Economic Union and Development Prospects for Canada (1985). *Report*. Volume I.

Maclean's (1989). "Special Report: Portrait of Two Nations." July 3. 23-82.

Magun, S. (1986). "The Effects of Canada-US Free Trade on the Canadian Labour Market." Canadian Economics Association Meeting. May 29.

Magun, S., Rao, S., and Lodh, B. (1988). "Impact of Canada-US Free Trade on the Canadian Economy." *Economic Council of Canada Discussion Paper* No. 331. August.

Purcell, S. K. (1981/2). "Mexico-US relations." *Foreign Affairs*. 59. 379-392.

Rashish, M. (1981). "North American economic relations." *Department of State Bulletin*. 81. 24-28.

Reynolds, C. W. and McCleery, R. K. (1985). "Modeling US-Mexico economic linkages." *American Economic Review*. 75, 2. 217-222

Rugman, A. M. (1988). "The Patterns of Bilateral Foreign Investment." In McKee, D. L. (ed.), *Canadian-American Economic Relations: Conflict and Cooperation on a Continental*. Praeger. 181-198.

Schott, J. (ed.) (1989). "More free-trade areas?" *Analysis in International Economics*. #27. Institute for International Economics, Washington DC.

Schott, J. J. (1988). "The Free Trade Agreement: A US Assessment." In Schott, J. J. and Smith, M. G. (eds.), *The Canada-United States Free Trade Agreement: The Global Impact*. Institute for International Economics. 1-35.

Schott, J. J. and Smith, M. G. (1988). "Services and Investment." In Schott, J. J. and Smith, M. G. (eds.), *The Canada-United States Free Trade Agreement: The Global Impact*. Institute for International Economics. 137-150.

Smith, C. (1988). "Zone of confusion: Tokyo study groups in a muddle over a Japan-US free-trade zone." *Far Eastern Economic Review*. 142, 41. 84-85.

Smith, P. H. (1989). *Global politics and the future of US-Mexican relations*. Presentation at a panel on "The future of US-Mexican relations." Latin American Studies Association. XV International congress, Miami.

Stokes, B. (1987). "Mexican momentum." *National Journal*. 27 June. 572-578.

Strodes, J. (1988). "O Canada! Gimme a Break!" *Financial World* August 23. 16-17.

Trigueros, I. (1989). "A free-trade area between Mexico and the United States." In Schott, J. (ed.) *Free trade areas and U.S. Foreign Policy*. Institute for International Economics. 255-270.

Verleger, P. K., Jr. (1988). "Implications of the Energy Provisions." In Schott, J. J. and Smith, M. G. (eds.), *The Canada-United States Free Trade Agreement: The Global Impact*. Institute for International Economics. 137-150.

Weintraub, S. (1984). *Free trade between Mexico and the United States?* Brookings Institution.

Whenmouth, E. (1989). "Japan as a trade buddy?" *Industry Week*. February 6. 61-62.

Williamson, J. (1990). "The progress of policy reform in Latin America." *Policy Analysis in International Economics*. 28. 25-78. Institute for International Economics, Washington DC.

Wonnacott, P. (1987). *The United States and Canada: The Quest for Free Trade: An Examination of Selected Issues*. Institute for International Economics.

———. (1988). "The Auto Sector." In Schott, J. J. and Smith, M. G. (eds.), *The Canada-United States Free Trade Agreement: The Global Impact*. Institute for International Economics. 137-150.

3

Global Markets in International Trade

Lawrence R. Klein

As the world shifted toward more open multilateral trading relationships after the Second World War and also completed the urgent tasks of reconstruction, there was a flowering of economic performance that was closely associated with the expansion of trade volume. By 1968 and 1969, trade volume expanded at rates in excess of 10%. Gross world product grew at rates between 4 and 6% for most of the decade of the 1960s and finished, just before recessionary forces were felt, at 5.4% in 1969.

Trade growth slowed considerably during the 1970s and also fluctuated. There were swings from plus to minus values in the early 1980s. The severe world recession of 1981-82 was associated with falling trade volume in each of these two years. By 1988 and 1989 volume expansion picked up again toward the high levels reached during the golden years of the 1960s.

In trying to look ahead, for the rest of this century, it does not appear that world trade volume is ready to grow for extended periods at rates above 10%, but respectable rates of about 5% do seem to be attainable. There are some powerful new developments taking place in the world economy that lend support to the idea that trade will be expansive.

In the first place the enhancement of the Common Market in Europe will undoubtedly contribute to increased trade volume, certainly among the European partners. It remains to be seen how this institutional change will affect trade between members and non-members of the Common Market. A second force, making for increased trade volume is the incorporation of Eastern Europe and the Soviet Union into the international trading system. These countries are staking their growth prospects on strong trade, by which they hope to acquire more goods/services, better quality items, and new-technology items. These acquisitions are viewed as means to an end—the achievement of living standards that are much closer to the Western norm.

The CMEA constituted a trading bloc that did not live up to its promise, and liberal multilateral trade is now viewed by the member countries as a new promising route, and it will undoubtedly bring more trade. In 1987 intra-bloc trade in the CMEA group constituted about 5.5% of total world trade.

A similar liberal strategy was followed by China after 1978, and there has been a significant trade expansion. This is part of the "open door" policy. It was moving smartly, until the political disturbances of June, 1989, occurred. Now we are witnessing a reassessment of openness both on the part of China and her trading partners, but it seems likely that expanded economic interactions with partners will gradually resume again.

All the recent developments have not, however, been positive. The oil embargo of 1973-74 and the associated "oil shocks" of 1973-74/1979-81 helped to de-stabilize the smooth growth of trade volume and accompanying production. Slower growth and erratic growth featured the international economy of the 1970s.

The LDC debt problem grew out of the petrol surplus. It was recycled through the medium of the world banking system in such a way that a crisis occurred, and this event, together with energy shocks have restrained trade volume expansion, even to this day. Nevertheless, there are reasons to be more optimistic about world trade and overall world economic activity once again. The spirit of the European boom is contagious, and this should help to open the trading community in the years ahead.

Some Possible Trading Patterns

There are many subdivisions in the world economy, but three that are crucial for understanding trade patterns and their evolution during the next few years are Europe, North America, and the Asia-Pacific.

By "Europe," I mean, obviously, the Common Market. It accounted for 22.3% of world trade in 1987. But now the term *Europe* is taking on a wider meaning. The opening of Europe to the East is such a striking event and has generated such enthusiasm that the Common Market cannot avoid the establishment of new ties with the six CMEA countries in Eastern Europe (Bulgaria, Czechoslovakia, East Germany, Hungary, Poland, and Romania). The position of the Soviet Union is unclear, but there will probably be closer economic/trade ties than at any time since the 1917 Revolution.

But the Common Market has much more in common with the nations of EFTA. Indeed, some EFTA members may join the EEC in the not-too-distant future. First we might look for expansion toward one Europe, embracing both EEC and EFTA countries; then the CMEA Six are likely to be drawn into the European economic environment. This is why we should eventually look toward one Europe. For the moment, the principal trading bloc in Europe will be the EEC, and this will be a formidable economic entity. Also, the population figures are impressive. The main driving force for economic cohesion in this area will be the Single Market, from January 1, 1993. The economic power of this concept is already impressive in contributing to the economic boom now occurring in Europe in preparation for the Single Market. We find strong production growth, larger trade volume, not bad inflation performance, and steady exchange rates.

The second area to consider is *North America*, where Canada and the United States have already started to form a free trade zone. Mexico has been reluctant to get too closely involved with two giant neighbors in North America but is now reconsidering and leaning toward completing the pact for the North American area.

When the idea of a free trade zone between Canada and the United States was being put to an actual vote and not simply being discussed in principle, there was substantial opposition in Canada. In the end, the fears generated by the opposition—that the United States would dominate Canada—were overcome and Canada approved the agreement, based on hopes that there would be gains from trade. I shall return below to the reasoning that lies behind the expectations of gains.

It was not surprising that Mexico showed little interest, or even opposition, to such a pact by the two industrial neighbors. But Mexico now has a different attitude toward trade policy. There has been frustration and disappointment with performance of the resource-rich economy. The debt burden, inflation dangers, and failed policies for achievement of economic stability have led to reconsideration of the possibilities of making gains from trade. In a sense, Mexico is turning toward policies of more openness, much as socialist countries have introduced open door policies in order to gain access to new technologies and some important consumer goods in order to provide citizens with significantly improved living conditions. Now, there is a real possibility of fashioning a North American Common Market.

US trade with Canada ranks among the largest bilateral flows anywhere in the world; so very large magnitudes are at stake. US trade with Mexico has also been very important. When Mexico first encountered difficulties with debt service in 1982, the initial reaction was to reduce imports from the United States. The bilateral merchandise flow from the US to Mexico fell immediately from $17.8 billion in 1981 to $11.8 billion in 1982. This sharp decline, when combined with similar cutbacks in exports to Brazil and other troubled Latin debtors, was enough to unsettle recovery of the US economy from the 1980-82 recession by as much as six months. It was not until 1988 that Mexican trade recovered to its previous high point of 1981 and this slow recovery has been contributory to our large external deficit.

On the Mexican side, the United States is obviously a prime export market, but that is only part of the story. Immigration, temporary or long-term, provides an enormous income flow for Mexico. At the same time the US is able to tap an inexpensive labor supply. The success of the *maquiladoras*—border industries with large tariff concessions—provides productive services at favorable costs to the United States. They constitute, by themselves, a limited free trade zone.

The free flows of goods and services among Canada, the United States, and Mexico hold out much promise. Canadian economists have estimated impressive gains for Canada as a result of production on a large scale for the enhanced market, the acquisition of Yankee know-how, and the elimination of delays in cross-border shipping.[1] There may be other gains, and they are all estimated to bring about significant increases in productivity. It remains to be seen if the Canadian studies are accurate. The gains have not yet been realized; it is much too early to see the benefits. In many respects, the gains estimated for the Canada-US ties are like those estimated for the Common Market in Europe after January 1, 1993.

The third region to be considered is the *Asia-Pacific* area. The major trading nations in this area deal in worldwide networks, and they have shown great reluctance to limit themselves to Pacific specialization, but the success of the European Common Market has led to reconsideration, especially because of fears that Europe may try to concentrate more on internal associations to the relative exclusion of outsiders. Also, at the present time when Western Europe has become so interested in expanding ties with Eastern Europe, Japan has looked at this possibility of building connections with the former socialistic countries but openly expressed the view that there is, so much potential, so many natural cultural ties, with China and East Asia, that they plan to focus attention there.

At the time that the Common Market in Europe was originally formed, Australia and New Zealand feared being squeezed from traditional markets where, as members of the British Commonwealth they had enjoyed favoritism in the UK market for their primary products. The concerns of Australia and New Zealand were, in fact, justified, but they found new outlets in the Asia-Pacific areas and are becoming more and more integrated there, in place of their old connections.

Within the Pacific Basin, there is a high degree of complementarity. Agricultural goods come from many countries. Australia and New Zealand can supply large quantities of grain, livestock products, and other agricultural items (food and non-food). Thailand is a leading rice exporter. There are other sources of food stuffs in the area; the Philippines can supply many tropical products.

Indonesia, with some help from Brunei and Malaysia, is a major energy supplier. There are many other raw materials—metals, rubber, forest products, etc.—available in abundant supply in the region. These are generally wanted, but they provide input for the industrial base, which is so important in Japan, South Korea, Taiwan, and other places too.

It is evident that there is an excellent "fit" among the economies of South East Asia and the Pacific. A natural reaction is for the partners in this "fit" to turn toward one another as the Common Market structure becomes more formidable. The "talk" about the concept of an Asian trading bloc in the form of a competing Common Market is no longer "ivory tower" speculation. It is fast becoming a reality.

These three trading zones constitute the main trading blocs in the world today. Not all trading blocs are successful. The Andean Pact countries and those of the Latin America Free Trade agreement are not powerful forces in world trade developments. There has not been a formation of a cohesive trading bloc in the Pacific, but a new situation is developing that makes it even more likely for the Asia-Pacific countries to band together.

Some Quantitative Magnitudes

There are big changes in prospect for the world trading system. The elimination of barriers in Europe—covering EEC members, new linkages between East and West, and possible agreements between EEC and EFTA countries—will surely re-orient trade and, very likely, increase its volume. Other changes in the main trading zones are in the offing and may have similar results, but it is useful to see where we stand now, at the beginning of these changes to come. Accordingly, I have extracted some relevant statistics from *Directions of Trade*, for presentation in Tables 3.1 and 3.2.

It should be remarked that there are many overlapping sources of trade statistics. Individual countries publish regular reports with many bilateral flows. There are multilateral reports by the UN Statistical Office, OECD, GATT, EEC and other sources. I have chosen to use IMF statistics from the *Directions of Trade* as a single homogenous source. The differences in valuation, country classification, and definition (FOB, FAS, or CIF) are not so important, either between or within sources because the points of reference and emphasis here are the broad differences among areas associated with magnitudes of trade flows. These differences are largely invariant with respect to finer points of measurement.

Table 3.1 is oriented around the three dominant countries—dominant in the world economy generally and dominant in each of the trade zones that are likely to be the most important. The US will be the "anchor" for North

Table 3.1 Some World Trade Flows for 1988 (merchandise in billions of US$)

US exports to:			US imports from:		
	World	$320.4		World	$459.9
	Japan	37.7		Japan	93.2
	Germany	14.3		Germany	27.4
	Canada	69.2		Canada	81.4
	Mexico	20.6		Mexico	23.5
	LDC	118.1		LDC	177.7
	EEC	75.9		EEC	88.7
Japan exports to:	World	265.0	Japan imports from:	World	187.5
	US	90.2		US	42.3
	Germany	15.8		Germany	8.1
	UK	10.6		UK	4.2
	LDC	102.0		LDC	91.5
	EEC	47.2		EEC	24.2
Germany exports to:	World	323.4	Germany imports from:	World	250.6
	US	26.0		US	16.6
	Japan	7.5		Japan	16.2
	UK	30.1		UK	17.4
	LDC	52.3		LDC	48.0
	EEC	176.0		EEC	129.8

Source: Directions of Trade, 1989.

American, Japan for the Asia-Pacific area, and Germany for the EEC. It is possible that the United States and Canada will join a Pacific institution as well as a greater North American free trade area.

First, we can see that the US is still the leading trading nation in the world, in terms of volume (value), although it is not the most open economy. Germany comes very close to the US in total export value depending on what exchange rates are used, but, unfortunately, the US more than offsets any possible German export edge with a very large import bulge.

The predominance of the US-Canadian trade is clearly visible in Table 3.1, but the US trade flows are very large with Japan, the developing world, and the EEC. In all cases there is a large import surplus. These figures show that while the import surplus with Japan is the largest listed, it is, by no means, the only surplus. The emphasis should be for the United States to improve the overall balance and not simply the bilateral balance vis-á-vis Japan. Preoccupation with the bilateral balance by policymakers is surely blatant mercantilism.

Germany has large trade-flow relationships with all the countries or areas listed, except possibly Japan, where its trade is carried on only at a moderate level. Germany is a dominant participant in the EEC and has large

Table 3.2 World Trade Flows with Some Trade Areas for 1988 (merchandise in billions of US$)

World exports to:	EEC	$1,045.5	World Exports from:	EEC $1,062.3	
World exports to:	Asia (LDC)	346.3	World imports from:	Asia (LDC)	371.0
	Japan	167.0		Japan	275.9
	Australia	32.9		Australia	35.4
	New Zealand	6.4		NewZealand	9.4
World exports to:	USA	437.4	World imports from:	USA	341.6
	Canada	101.1		Canada	113.8
	Mexico	27.3		Mexico	32.0
World exports to:	USSR*	68.0	World imports from:	USSR*	65.1
	Poland	16.2		Poland	17.6
	Hungary	8.7		Hungary	10.4
	Romania	9.2		Romania	14.1

Total World exports $2,7075

* Includes other non-members of IMF who were allied to USSR

Source: Directions of Trade, 1989.

export-import volumes vis-á-vis Netherlands, Belgium, Italy, France, Switzerland, and UK (listed in Table 3.1). Both Japan and the United States are more involved than is Germany in trade with developing countries.

Japan's trade is distributed throughout the world. The United States is a major partner and much larger than the entire EEC. This pattern may well change in the near future, with Japan trying to make a larger showing in Europe. The developing world is very important for Japan, and within this area the main activity is in trade between Japan and Asian developing countries. This includes more than just the Pacific Basin.

Turning to world flows in Table 3.2, we see that the EEC is a very formidable trading area. The exports or imports amounted to approximately 40% of total world trade.

World exports to Asia, developing plus developed, are only about one-half those to the EEC. On the world import side, the proportion is larger, about two-thirds. North American trade with the world is only about one-half that of the Common Market. If there is a tendency for the world pattern to split among these three groups, it is clear that the Common Market will begin a new era with a size advantage. If Canada and the United States ally themselves with the Pacific Basin, that will alter the balance toward equality, but a unified total Europe will be a stronger competitor.

The figures in Table 3.2 show how small the CMEA has been in world trade. A main change in the volumes of trading relationships is likely to be centered on the relationship between East and West Europe. There is room for considerable expansion here. It remains to be seen how much North America or the Asia-Pacific area can penetrate the external relationships of Eastern Europe and also help to make the volume of the latter grow. Japan has suggested that their main economic interests lie in Asia, especially with China, and may cultivate an expansion in that direction more than in Europe. There is ample room for Asian trade expansion together with European expansion in the total world economy.

Trading Zones

The world is moving in the direction of the establishment of trading zones held together by bilateral agreements or by a strong institutional framework, as in the case of the EEC, headquartered in Brussels. The members of the Common Market, by and large, like the performance of their organization. It is deemed a success. More countries want to join. Austria and Norway are two possible new members. Other countries like Turkey and Israel want to join but are not allowed membership. Whether other countries would reap economic benefits from the gains of trade or whether they have a political agenda that makes membership highly desirable, it is sometimes difficult to tell, but outsiders do definitely want to be accepted.

The Common Market organization is projecting strong gains as a result of establishment of the Single Market after January 1, 1993. These projections are subject to error, but planning is going ahead as though they will prove to be accurate. The embryonic or planned ventures elsewhere are being projected on just about the same basis as the EEC case.

There are reasons for questioning the wisdom of going ahead, at full speed, along this route. In the United States, thinking was originally directed at another approach after the Second World War, namely along the lines of multilateral free trade. This objective appeared to work extremely well in the 1950s and 1960s. Bilateral agreements, restrictions on trade, barter arrangements for bulk commodities, and other illiberal practices were a carry-over from the emergency conditions of the war. Steps toward the multilateral free trade goal were instrumental in setting the world on a vigorous growth path, both for production and trade volume. The formation of regional blocs can be viewed as a deviation from the goal of multilateral free trade.

At the theoretical level, it can be shown that under the usual kinds of assumptions made in welfare economics, a complete free trade system is *optimal*, albeit in a special sense, namely, the sense of Pareto optimality. This is not a strong criterion, but it is the best that can be attained, and that is only in *theoretical* terms. The establishment of a few subsystems, each of which breaks down internal barriers on a regional basis, may provide steps toward the multilateral ideal, but not necessarily so. If the blocs retaliate against each other and carry on economic warfare the world may turn out to be much worse off. If there is trade *diversion* (say, to the EEC) instead of trade *creation*, the establishment of a few strong trading blocs can be quite perverse. To the extent that a North American bloc and an Asia-Pacific bloc are created in response to ambitious expansion of the Common Market, we encounter all the bad fears of the workings of the more elaborate institutional system.

On the whole, trading zones have not been successful. The Common Market does seem to bring something special to Europe, but the CMEA and LAFTA were not known for their economic successes in establishing good foreign trade institutions. The CMEA is such a failure that it may not survive the upheavals in Eastern Europe. It did not have a sensible pricing system, and it did not provide high-class goods to the vast consuming population in the Soviet Union and Eastern Europe. The data show in Table 3.2, that CMEA trade has not been a force in the World Economy, nor a mechanism for generating good living conditions in member countries. On the other hand, the members of CMEA want now to join Western organizations and to realize more gains from trade.

As early as the 1960s, the Soviet Union knew that it needed trade, just to provide food during a bad harvest season and to bring new technologies to have an improved output flow. Soviet trade with the West began to expand towards the end of the '60s, but it was not truly liberalized. Now, there is a full understanding that the Eastern European countries and the USSR will have to import Western technology and quality goods. To pay for these imports, it will be necessary to get financial capital from abroad and also increase exports. This requires improved economic efficiency and may imply abandonment of the CMEA framework, in the light of political transformation in the area.

At the close of the Second World War, the Soviet Union and some of the countries of Eastern Europe had the chance to join GATT and the two Bretton Woods financial organizations, the World Bank and the IMF. They opted for their own regional apparatus, and it did not work; now they want belated entry into the Western organizations. It is unlikely that the East European countries will try to reconstruct their trading bloc. They will, in the first place, construct their new trading relationships with the West, and some may eventually join an expanded EEC. Some are already in the IMF and World Bank on a limited basis. Their first steps appear to be to seek wider and closer ties with these world multilateral organizations. They will then be in a position to consider EEC membership if it is offered sometime in the future.

Countries of the Andean Pact or LAFTA have many serious domestic problems. Their internal economies will have to be put in order before they can consider the formation of trading blocs because countries experiencing hyperinflation will surely find it difficult to lay out any sensible formulas for mutual cooperation.

Some Projections of World Trade

Project LINK has been used for more than 20 years to study the international economy—production, trade, exchange rates, the international transmission mechanism (see Tables 3.3, 3.4, 3.5, 3.6, and 3.7).

Since 1987, we have noted a strong pick up in the growth rate of real world exports (or imports). The gain in 1988, at 8.3%, was so strong that it caught the LINK forecasters by surprise. It was reminiscent of the powerful expansion of the late 1960s, when the rate sometimes exceeded 10%. The three years 1987, 1988, and 1989 were all favorable (5.7, 8.3, and 7.9%, respectively).

The 1980s were not impressive for trade growth until the very end. The present LINK projections do not foresee a return to the choppy patterns of the 1980s, but project a fairly steady expansion in the range of 4 to 6% annually. A cyclical correction may have been in order, but the new developments in Europe find the expansionary forces outweighing the contractionary forces. At the present time, 1990 and possibly 1991, there is a slowing down period to deal with the adjustment process. Some countries will go through actual recessions, while others will be stimulated by trying to further the restructuring of markets in reform areas.

There is still a debt overhang in many developing countries, and the Far East economies are experiencing some inflationary pressure, as well as competitiveness from Europe and North America. In the end, LINK projects a world economy that gets reasonably soon to a 3% growth path for output, nurtured by a trade expansion that is between 5 and 6% after a slowdown in 1990. There is moderate inflationary pressure and some improvement in unemployment, especially in the EEC.

The Japanese and German current account surpluses are not wiped out, but they are reduced in this projection. The Japanese balance should contract faster than Germany's. Against these gains, it should be noted that the UK and Spain deteriorate. The United States realizes some gains. They are almost dramatic for the net export balance of goods and services in the national income accounts but not so dramatic for the current account because government interest payments abroad keep these deficits from being reduced very much.

There will have to be growing import surpluses in Eastern Europe and the Soviet Union, as part of the restructuring. This must go on for a few years, at least.

Table 3.3 World Exports, Imports, and Trade Balances (f.o.b., in billions of US$) Project LINK—United Nations/DIESA

Pre-meeting forecast, Spring 1990

	1989	%chg	1990	%chg	1991	%chg	1992	%chg	1993	%chg	1994	%chg
Developed Market Economies												
Exports	2168.74	8.4	2400.67	10.7	2645.48	10.2	2915.42	10.2	3213.71	10.2	3529.72	9.8
Imports	2203.26	9.7	2450.95	11.2	2693.24	9.9	2955.22	9.7	3248.96	9.9	3575.97	10.1
Balance	-34.52		-50.28		-47.76		-39.80		-35.25		-46.25	
North-America												
Exports	492.20	14.1	527.27	7.1	581.19	10.2	643.76	10.8	716.64	11.3	789.23	10.1
Imports	599.98	8.8	634.58	5.8	685.16	8.0	744.6	8.7	808.60	8.6	873.89	8.1
Balance	-107.78		-107.31		-103.98		-100.84		-91.96		-84.66	
Developed East												
Exports	316.93	5.6	333.37	5.2	359.92	8.0	390.71	8.6	421.15	7.8	454.52	7.9
Imports	241.86	18.1	263.10	8.8	289.92	10.2	319.59	10.2	351.32	9.9	390.10	11.0
Balance	75.07		70.27		70.00		71.12		69.83		64.43	
EEC												
Exports	1137.14	7.2	1292.28	13.6	1435.31	11.1	1584.44	10.4	1751.64	10.6	1934.84	10.5
Imports	1144.02	9.3	1310.50	14.6	1455.42	11.1	1601.81	10.1	1773.12	10.7	1964.80	10.8
Balance	-6.88		-18.22		-20.10		-17.37		-21.47		-29.96	
Rest of Industrialized												
Exports	222.47	6.6	247.75	11.4	269.06	8.6	296.50	10.2	324.27	9.4	351.13	8.3
Imports	217.40	5.9	242.77	11.7	262.74	8.2	289.22	10.1	315.92	9.2	347.19	9.9
Balance	5.07		4.98		6.32		7.29		8.35		3.95	
Developing Countries												
Exports	729.68	15.0	790.94	8.4	875.16	10.6	970.73	10.9	1078.01	11.1	1203.66	11.7
Imports	687.24	12.6	756.08	10.0	833.16	10.2	923.29	10.8	1025.47	11.1	1145.84	11.7
Balance	42.43		34.85		41.99		47.44		52.54		57.82	
Latin America, Caribbean												
Exports	115.63	7.8	123.47	6.8	132.74	7.5	143.93	8.4	156.11	8.5	170.49	9.2
Imports	91.66	6.1	97.08	5.9	104.92	8.1	114.43	9.1	125.83	10.0	140.81	11.9
Balance	23.97		26.39		27.83		29.49		30.29		29.68	

(Continues)

Table 3.3 (Continued)

Pre-meeting forecast, Spring 1990

	1989	%chg	1990	%chg	1991	%chg	1992	%chg	1993	%chg	1994	%chg
Africa												
Exports	61.41	15.3	64.38	4.8	69.29	7.6	75.37	8.8	81.80	8.5	89.76	9.7
Imports	69.46	7.9	73.99	6.5	79.46	7.4	86.18	8.5	93.69	8.7	101.64	8.5
Balance	-8.05		-9.61		-10.17		-10.81		-11.89		-11.88	
South, East Asia												
Exports	359.37	14.6	394.60	9.8	445.12	12.8	500.20	12.4	563.06	12.6	636.61	13.1
Imports	346.20	17.4	388.64	12.3	435.99	12.2	488.52	12.0	548.85	12.3	619.61	12.9
Balance	13.17		5.97		9.13		11.68		14.21		17.00	
China												
Exports	52.50	10.6	57.92	10.3	64.24	10.9	71.53	11.3	79.49	11.1	89.18	12.2
Imports	56.22	7.0	61.07	8.6	66.46	8.8	73.11	10.0	81.49	11.5	90.86	11.5
Balance	-3.73		-3.15		-2.21		-1.58		-2.00		-1.69	
West Asia												
Exports	85.68	29.4	91.36	6.6	99.08	8.5	108.94	9.9	120.26	10.4	133.01	10.6
Imports	73.05	9.9	79.60	9.0	86.34	8.5	94.12	9.0	103.29	9.7	114.03	10.4
Balance	12.63		11.76		12.74		14.82		16.97		18.98	
Mediterranean												
Exports	27.78	3.0	30.06	8.2	32.80	9.1	36.17	10.3	38.92	7.6	42.75	9.8
Imports	34.22	8.0	37.72	10.2	40.31	6.9	45.12	11.9	48.42	7.3	52.66	8.8
Balance	-6.44		-7.66		-7.51		-8.95		-9.50		-9.91	
C.P.E.												
Exports	229.25	2.2	244.18	6.5	255.51	4.6	269.68	5.5	288.13	6.8	306.58	6.4
Imports	233.73	2.4	248.76	6.4	270.38	8.7	293.33	8.5	317.16	8.1	335.88	5.9
Balance	-4.47		-4.58		-14.88		-23.66		-29.03		-29.30	
World Exports	3127.67	9.4	3435.78	9.9	3776.14	9.9	4155.82	10.1	4579.82	10.2	5039.91	10.0
World Export Price	3.88	1.3	4.10	5.7	4.29	4.6	4.48	4.4	4.67	4.2	4.88	4.5
World Exports real	805.37	7.9	837.22	4.0	879.61	5.1	927.51	5.4	980.72	5.7	1032.89	5.3
Stat. Discrep.	0.54		24.98		24.95		20.73		11.69		17.68	

Table 3.4 Growth Rates of World Gross National Product (based on 1970 US$) Project LINK—United Nations/DIESA

Pre-meeting forecast, Spring 1990

	1989	1990	1991	1992	1993	1994	Mean
Developed Market Economies	3.5	2.5	3.1	3.0	3.1	3.1	3.0
North America	2.9	1.8	2.6	2.6	2.9	2.8	2.6
Developed East	4.9	4.3	4.2	4.1	4.2	4.4	4.3
EEC	3.8	3.0	3.5	3.2	3.2	3.0	3.3
Rest of Industrialized	2.1	1.2	0.6	1.9	1.5	1.7	1.5
Developing Countries	3.5	3.7	4.7	5.2	5.2	5.4	4.6
Latin American, Caribbean	1.1	1.4	2.9	3.8	4.2	4.9	3.0
Africa	2.4	2.6	2.3	2.9	3.1	3.1	2.7
South, East Asia	6.3	6.0	6.2	6.1	6.0	6.2	6.1
China	3.9	5.1	6.1	6.5	6.5	6.4	5.7
West Asia	6.0	4.4	4.7	5.1	4.3	3.8	4.7
Mediterranean	1.2	0.7	4.3	6.0	4.9	4.9	3.7
C.P.E.	0.3	-0.4	0.1	1.1	1.0	0.5	0.4
World Total	2.9	2.3	2.9	3.1	3.2	3.1	2.9

Table 3.5 Growth Rates of Per Capita World Gross National Product (based on 1970 US$) Project LINK—United Nations/DIESA

Pre-meeting forecast, Spring 1990

	1989	1990	1991	1992	1993	1994	Mean
Developed Market Economies	3.0	2.0	2.6	2.5	2.7	2.6	2.6
North America	2.0	0.9	1.8	1.8	2.1	1.9	1.8
Developed East	4.3	3.7	3.6	3.6	3.6	3.8	3.8
EEC	3.8	2.9	3.4	3.1	3.2	3.0	3.2
Rest of Industrialized	1.7	0.8	0.2	1.5	1.2	1.3	1.1
Developing Countries	1.8	2.0	3.0	3.5	3.5	3.7	2.9
Latin America, Caribbean	-0.7	-0.6	1.0	1.8	2.2	2.9	1.1
Africa	-0.4	-0.2	-0.5	0.2	0.3	0.4	0.0
South, East Asia	4.5	4.2	4.6	4.5	4.4	4.5	4.4
China	2.7	3.8	4.9	5.3	5.3	5.2	4.5
West Asia	3.5	1.6	2.1	2.4	1.6	1.1	2.0
Mediterranean	0.0	-0.3	3.1	4.8	3.8	3.7	2.5
C.P.E.	-0.4	-1.1	-0.5	0.4	0.3	-0.1	-0.2
World Total	2.2	1.5	2.2	2.4	2.5	2.4	2.2

Table 3.6 OECD Unemployment Rate (in percentages) Project LINK—United Nations/DIESA

	1989	1990	1991	1992	1993	1994	Mean
OECD	6.2	6.5	6.4	6.3	6.0	5.9	6.2
North America	5.4	5.8	5.8	5.6	5.2	5.1	5.5
Developed East	2.8	2.9	3.1	3.2	3.5	3.8	3.2
EEC	9.9	10.0	9.9	9.6	9.5	9.3	9.7
Rest of OECD	5.7	6.0	6.3	6.8	6.6	6.2	6.3

Note: Excl. Greece, Iceland, Netherlands, and Switzerland.

Table 3.7 Percentage of Change in OECD Private Consumption Deflator (inflation rate in local currency weighted with GNP in current US$) Project LINK—United Nations/DIESA

Pre-meeting forecast Spring 1990

	1989	1990	1991	1992	1993	1994	Mean
OECD	3.7	4.0	3.9	3.9	3.8	3.3	3.8
North America	4.4	4.1	4.5	4.9	4.6	5.0	4.6
Developed East	3.1	2.6	2.9	2.9	2.8	2.6	2.8
EEC	3.5	4.1	3.9	3.8	3.7	3.1	3.7
Rest of OECD	4.6	5.2	4.8	3.7	3.6	3.5	4.2

Trade is going to play a very important role in the world economy of the 1990s. It should basically be a good recovery period, to deal with present world problems. The standard projection is one of steady, modest growth, with pockets of need in parts of the developing world and in Eastern Europe, but there is a good possibility that this projection may be understating the course of economic progress. The usual arguments that rely on technological advance of an extraordinary nature and on the job ahead for restructuring could, by themselves, generate a stronger expansion, but there is something altogether new on the horizon, namely, the fact that the Cold War is over and, for a time at least, the world could reap some "Peace Dividends," which could aid as much as 0.5% to the rate of output expansion. The corresponding world trade expansion would probably be higher—by at least one full percentage point.

References

Dungan, Peter and Thomas Wilson, "The Macroeconomic Effects of the Canada-US Free Trade Agreement," Institute for Policy Analysis, University of Toronto, November, 1988 (working paper DP88-18).

4

The European Community, EFTA, and the New Europe

Peter W. Ludlow

Introduction

The EC is frequently cited as the most advanced example of a new generation of trading blocks which will eventually determine (or distort) the character of the multilateral trading system. As such it has been taken as a possible "model" (or warning) for those in North America who favor a North American Economic Community. The EC is not, however, the only nor even the most relevant model in Western Europe. There is another: the EC-EFTA bloc, or, as it is now officially called, the European Economic Space.

The EC, whatever certain political leaders may still pretend to the contrary, was from the beginning an adventure in supranationalism: an enterprise founded on economic integration but committed to political union. As such, its counterpart in North America is, this paper suggests, not the US-Canada Free Trade Area, still less a broader Northern American grouping, but the United States of America. For obvious reasons the United States of Europe—if and when they emerge—on the basis of the European Community will be very different from the United States of America. But comparisons are not entirely misleading.

EFTA, by contrast, represented from its earliest days an effort to maximize free trade, while allowing its member states their separate sovereignties. Viewed from several important angles, their collective achievement has been remarkable. They have progressively liberalized their trade with each other and with the rest of the world. They have also, in many important respects, maintained their differences, and in doing so enriched European political society as a whole. The Nordic welfare states and Swiss direct democracy cannot be copied 100% elsewhere, but they have over the years enlarged Europeans' sense of what can or should be done in politics and society. Finally, and by no means least, they have prospered. Measured by any yardstick, the EFTA states are amongst the wealthiest not only in Europe, but in the world.

And yet, viewed from another angle, the history of EFTA is one long story of retreat, accompanied as at present by soul-searching domestic political debates which appear to call into question the continuing viability not only of EFTA as a group, but even of its component parts. The recurrent focus of these periodic bouts of collective doubt is, it need hardly be said, the European Community. Without the EC, EFTA would never have come into being. It has continued to be its *raison d'etre* ever since: a magnet which has already drawn three of the original seven members, the UK, Denmark and Portugal; a threat which has induced a curious combination of well mannered despair and energetic diplomacy in defence of national independence and economic prosperity.

The contrasting experiences—and dynamics—of the two principal groups of Western European countries highlight many of the problems with which North Americans will be confronted as they attempt to reshape their own economic and political relations. So too do the efforts of the EC and EFTA to forge what is now officially called the European Economic Space. All these problems are, however, also interesting in their own right, because the decisions which are taken regarding both the future of the EC and EFTA can now be seen to be of fundamental, strategic importance for the development of Europe as a whole.

The first part of this paper looks at the development of the EC, revisiting some of the problems that were so vigorously debated by American political scientists in the 1960s and 1970s. What kind of venture is the EC? What lessons can we glean about its dynamics which provide us with a clue to its future?

The second section deals with EFTA, and still more with the efforts of its member states to come to terms with the EC reality. It concludes with some speculative remarks about the outcome of the current EC-EFTA negotiations on the European Economic Space.

The third section relates this Western European debate to the broader problem of the future of Europe as a whole. Until 1989, EC-EFTA relations could be considered as an interesting, and possibly even an important chapter in the reorganization of West-West, nevertheless, in the post-American era. With the collapse of the Communist regimes of Eastern

Europe, however, the dialogue between EC and EFTA has assumed an altogether greater significance. If the EC and EFTA can together work out a *modus vivendi* which respects the political autonomy of the great unit, but guarantees to the smaller group the economic benefits of integration and the continuing enjoyment of a limited, but real political independence, this could become a seminal factor in the determination of Europe's new architecture as a whole.

The European Community

The principal distinguishing feature of the European Community is that from the beginning it has been based on the assumption that the only way in which the national states of Western Europe could cope with the threats and challenges of the evolving international system was through a measured but nevertheless real redistribution of sovereignty from national to supranational level. The immediate and most enduring expression of this assumption was an institutional architecture consisting of a supranational Commission, a Council representing the member states, an Assembly or Parliament, and a Court of Justice, all collectively responsible for the formulation and administration of laws and policies which, once agreed upon, overrode the ambitions or interests of the individual member states. In the 1970s, two modifications to this structure were introduced which did not, in any way, call into question the original design, but which immensely enhanced its overall impact: the formalization of the link between the European Community institutions and the heads of government and state in the member states through the creation of the European Council and the introduction of direct elections to the European Parliament.

Early academic literature on the Community highlighted the functionalist strategy embodied in the treaties of the 1950s, concentrating as they did on specific sectors or problems: Coal and Steel, a Customs Union, or Atomic Energy policy. When the anticipated spillover to other sectors did not occur, or was disappointingly slow in transpiring, pessimists concluded that the Community method as such was misconceived. Judgements of this nature were based, however, on an unwarrantedly mechanistic theory which overemphasized the process, but underrated the durability of the institutions, and the continuing relevance of the assumptions that they embodied. It would, of course, be foolish to ignore the importance of increased integration and interdependence registered for example in the striking growth of intra-Community trade amongst the original Six in the 1950s and 1960s, and the no less dramatic transformation of the UK's trading patterns since the early 1970s. This impersonal and inexorable process is vital to the development of the European Community: it is not, however, unique to the members of the EC. EFTA states are in terms of their trading patterns thoroughly "communitaire."

The distinctive features of the history of the European Community are not to be found in the integration process itself, but in its political history, which like all political history involves the constant interplay of institutions, personalities, and interests, against the background of shifting challenges and threats both internally and externally. The European Community is a common market: it is also, still more importantly, an increasingly autonomous, organized political society.

There is no need in an essay of this character to give a step-by-step account of the European Community's evolution from its relatively humble origins as a coal and steel community in the early 1950s. It is, however, important to provide some concrete illustrations of the dynamics of the Community process and in particular of the central role of the institutions in the process. Coal and steel may pass away and even the CAP may be modified beyond recognition, but the institutions have over time developed an autonomy and robustness which have made them immune to the changing fortunes of particular policies or sectors.

The illustrations of the Community's essential character and dynamics that follow are inevitably selective. They are not, however, arbitrary. The first is, not surprisingly, the founding document of the Community itself, namely the Schuman Plan of May 9, 1950. The rest, however, come from the period of crisis when, in the 1970s and 1980s, a series of internal and external shocks seemed, even to some of those most closely involved with the Community, to threaten its existence. In reality, the crises vindicated the design forged in 1950.

As far as the Schuman Plan is concerned, a few quotations will suffice to illustrate the fundamental political objective of the exercise from the very beginning and the key role assigned to the High Authority, the forerunner of what is now the European Commission.

> The contribution which an organized and living Europe can bring to civilization is indispensable to the maintenance of peaceful relations . . . Europe will not be made all at once, or according to a single, general plan. It will be built through concrete achievements, which first create a *de facto* solidarity. The gathering of the nations of Europe requires the elimination of the age-old opposition of France and Germany. The first concern in any action undertaken must be these two countries.
>
> With this aim in view, the French Government proposes to take action immediately on one limited but decisive point. The French Government proposes to place Franco-German production of Coal and Steel under a common High Authority, within the framework of an organization open to the participation of the other countries of Europe . . . .
>
> By pooling basic production and by setting up a new High Authority whose decisions would be binding on France, Germany and other member

countries, this proposal will build the first concrete foundation of a European federation which is indispensable to the preservation of peace.

In subsequent years, much of the passion which informed this official document was diluted by the realities of every day. The basic philosophy and the institutions that reflected it survived, however, even when, as in the 1970s and 1980s, a global crisis struck and visions of European federation were, to say the least, somewhat dimmed.

The development of *monetary cooperation* within the EC provides an almost flawless example of the limitations of functionalist expectations of spillover, the consequent significance of external shock and internal political leadership, and the magnetic capacity of the central institutional structure of the Community to gather to itself new policy initiatives, even when they were as major as the European Monetary System.

There were, and there are, good theoretical reasons for thinking that the creation of a Customs Union will lead almost inevitably to economic and monetary union. The argument, frequently heard today in connection with the forthcoming intergovernmental conference on EMU, was set out in classical form in a League of Nations study published in 1947.

> For a Customs Union to exist it is necessary to allow free movement of goods within the Union. For the Customs Union to be a reality it is necessary to allow free movement of persons. For a Customs Union to be stable it is necessary to maintain free exchangeability of currency and stable exchange rates within the Union. This implies, inter alia, free movement of capital within the Union. When there is free movement of goods, persons and capital in an area, diverse economic policies concerned with maintaining economic activity cannot be pursued.

In the course of the 1960s, the European Community of the Six went a long way toward creating a Customs Union. They advanced very little, however, toward an Economic and Monetary Union. Many explanations can be given. Two, closely related, are particularly important. The first is that the Treaty of Rome, presumably on the assumption that the development would be more or less automatic, did not spell out any very precise plans or obligations under this heading. The second, still more important, is that the European Customs Union developed within an international framework in which some of the most important attributes of a full Economic and Monetary Union, in particular exchange rate stability and discipline on states who deviate from the norms of good conduct, were guaranteed by a hegemonical power outside the European Community, namely the United States of America.

It is true that towards the end of the 1960s, to some extent in anticipation of the ending of the American system, the Community started to plan for

Economic and Monetary Union by 1980. The Werner Plan was nevertheless flawed, first because it set its sights unnecessarily high, and second, and still more importantly, because it did not tie in neatly with the institutional structure of the Community at that particular juncture. On the contrary, the economic and monetary experts of the European Community still gravitated naturally toward Washington and more particularly the IMF as a source of leadership, and for assistance and discipline when things went wrong.

It took the crisis of the Bretton Woods system and all that followed, plus a major, sustained demonstration of political leadership by the German Chancellor, the French President, and, to a lesser extent, the President of the European Commission, to alter the situation and to launch the European Monetary System in 1977-1979. Once the new ground rules had been established at high political level, however, the operation of the System was rightly and inevitably entrusted to the experts who had been so unprepared at the end of the 1960s and were, in many cases, still very skeptical about the feasibility of the EMS at the time of its birth. The key committees which assumed responsibility for the System had already been in existence for 15 years. Once the political mandate was given to them in 1979, however, both the character and the impact of these two committees, the Monetary Committee and the Central Bank Governors' Committee began to change.

While it may still be true that central bankers within the Community and more particularly the President of the Bundesbank, are unlikely to be in the forefront of calls for radical departures, the Community framework has become increasingly important in their day-to-day policies and their stake in, at the very least, the maintenance of what we have has become more and more obvious. The *Eurofed* when it emerges in the course of the next five to ten years, will not be a creation *ex nihilo*. On the contrary, it will be the logical conclusion to a process in which the transfer of powers which its establishment will signal, have in fact been ceded more gradually, and through which the skills required to run it have been learned by those who at the beginning would have looked askance at any blueprint for a European Central Bank before the next century. Political signals to and through a part of the EC's institutional structure that was in many ways rather dormant have thus molded an unlikely group into a central element of the emergent government of Europe.

A further illustration of the way in which the established institutional structure of the Community came into its own as, at a given moment, external pressure and internal political leadership combined to confer on it powers which it had always in principle had under the original treaties, but which it had been unable to exercise can be found in the *new generation of business-oriented policies* that the EC developed from approximately 1980 onwards. The most important are, of course, the Single Market program itself; high technology programs such as ESPRIT, BRITE and RACE; and the new departures in Competition policy associated particularly with Commissioner Sutherland from 1985 onward.

As Lord Cockfield frequently emphasized, a great deal of the 1992 program for the creation of the internal market was as old as the Community itself. The Treaty of Rome is, after all, dedicated to the four freedoms: goods, services, capita,l and persons. Similarly, Commissioner Sutherland needed to look no further than the Treaty itself when he began to develop a much more ambitious set of competition policies in the mid-1980s. The framework was already there. What had changed in both cases was the external environment where, as a result of the increasing globalization of manufacturing industry and the financial markets, Community-level, as distinct from member state-level action seemed to a sufficient number of actors in both public life and the private sector increasingly essential. The Community institutions were there: they had the powers; they were mobilized.

The pattern emerges equally clearly in the sphere of technology. Under pressure in the new era of global competition, European business, which previously had had relatively little to do with European Community institutions, joined forces with one of the shrewdest Commissioners of the last 20 years, Viscount Davignon, to exploit the political potential of the Commission, in a situation in which national governments were perceived to be increasingly powerless. The technology example is a particularly good one since there was briefly serious competition between the supranational Community programs and the intergovernmental EUREKA program, which was open to EFTA members as well as EC states on an equal basis. As the last few years have proved, the intergovernmental strategy embodied in EUREKA, though not without some fruits, has been no match for the supranational Community, acting in coalition with powerful private interests looking for concrete results.

The final case history, namely the development of the *Community's external policies*, is still being played out, but once again it seems increasingly likely that the Community institutions fashioned 40 years ago will prove superior to the formidable efforts of members states' foreign services to limit their collective ventures in foreign policy to intergovernmental political cooperation. The story is a complex one, but its principal features may be characterized in the following terms. The communities have always had an external dimension—inevitably, since provisions transforming the relations between member states affect the external relations of the Community as a whole.

The Community institutions therefore quickly established their competence in external trade and development. From the Kennedy Round onward, the EC's negotiations have been conducted by the Commission, which has also concluded a large number of supplementary trade agreements with all and sundry.

Trade policy is, however, only a part and traditionally, in Europe at least, a somewhat unprestigious part of foreign policy. "Real" foreign policy continues to be made in the foreign and defence ministries of the member states. With the breakdown of the American system, however, there was even here an important evolution in the late 1960s and early 1970s resulting in the launching of European Political Cooperation.

Progress has been slower than in the monetary sphere: the American system institutionalized in NATO has, until recently at any rate, proved much more durable and therefore reinforced the inherent unreadiness of member states to sanction a transfer of powers to the European level in this sphere, as in others. There has, however, been movement, first in the direction of preventing unnecessary conflict or confusion between two types of Community policy, i.e., European Political Cooperation and the external policies of the Treaty-based Community. The Single European Act codified progress at this sphere, as in much else when it decreed that "the external policies of the European Community and the policies agreed in European Political Cooperation must be consistent," and specified a number of practical measures designed to advance the objective.

In calling for consistency, the Single European Act in effect sanctions separateness. Once again, however, external opportunity and internal political leadership created a situation in which the superior robustness and efficiency of the supranational system has increasingly asserted itself. In 1985, it was still possible in Paris, Bonn, and London to contemplate building up the intergovernmental system as an almost autonomous pillar in the European Community construction. In 1990, a majority of working diplomats in the foreign services of the member states probably still hope that a second route can be preserved and developed, but as Ambassador Froment-Meurice and I found when preparing our recent report on a common European Foreign Policy, the arguments put forward are somewhat less than convincing and the hopes of those who advance them bear rather little conviction. A combination of the "re-launching" of the European Community through the 1992 program and the Single European Act and a significant, voluntary and involuntary, reappraisal of their global priorities by the European Community's principal partners or neighbors, the US, the Soviet Union and Japan, has exposed the fundamental limitations of medium-sized powers such as France and the United Kingdom, and the corresponding opportunity of supranational institutions representing a much larger Community as a whole.

As a result, it is no longer simply idealistic to imagine a fully integrated European foreign policy, operated and controlled through the principal Treaty of Rome institutions, as another common policies of the Community already are. On the contrary, this is already, particularly with regard to the rapidly developing political and economic architecture of the new Europe, a reality rather than a fantasy. Policies decided in the Councils of ministers, more often than not on the proposal of the European Commission, with regard to Eastern Europe, the Soviet Union, not to mention EFTA are already more significant both in scope and operability than the piecemeal efforts of Mitterand, Thatcher, and Andreotti, not to mention their foreign ministries and even, outside the specific intra-German issue, of Chancellor Kohl and Mr. Genscher.

This rapid and inevitably rather impressionistic survey of some of the more important themes of the development of the European Community so far should have demonstrated that the original, political assumptions and objectives of those who launched the process in 1950 have remained at the center of the Community's development. The European Community is about the promotion of greater wealth through the liberalization of trade and the development of other common policies. It is an economic community. It has always however, been still more, a political venture; a sustained effort, first to modify the natural inclinations and unruly behavior of member states which had led to several disastrous wars, and second to mould the same states into a new political entity, variously defined in Community documents as a Federation or, more commonly, a Union.

Progress has not been tidy. Policy priorities have changed greatly over time, as the world has changed or attitudes toward economic management have modified. The European communities were born in a period when a great majority of policymakers, on both left and right, assigned the public purse a far more important role in economic management than their successors do today. Only 15 years ago, a working group set up by the European Commission on the role of public finance in European integration concluded that if the Community wished to develop even a "lightweight" federal structure, its budget would have to account for at least 7-1/2 to 10% of GDP. Today, even the most committed federalists would regard 5% as an outer limit.

Fashions have therefore changed. The institutional architecture and the philosophy that underlay it, by contrast, has remained a constant, pointing toward the long-term goal described by Schuman and providing a succession of political leaders with instruments to master very different situations internally and confront very different challenges externally. As with any political community, the EC has had good leaders and bad ones. It is no discredit to the strong or exoneration of the weak, however, to say that the system has been more important in the long run than any of them. Looking back, the Thorn years, which were in almost every respect depressingly undistinguished, will increasingly seem to fit into an extended process of power-accumulation by the Community institutions. By the same token, Jacques Delors' major achievement will probably be seen to have been his ability to grasp the fact that this cumulative process, coupled with the emergence of a new global political economy had decisively tilted the balance of opportunity between member states and Community institutions.

At the decisive moment in the autumn of 1985 when Delors convinced even the most reluctant Europeans that if they really wanted a Single Market they would have to sanction at least a partial restoration of the majority voting regime which had lain in abeyance since De Gaulle's intervention of 1965-1966, he did far more than ensure the achievement of the 1992 program. He initiated a process in which the inherent strengths of the institutions were unleashed in many areas of Community policy. Over the past five years, he and his colleagues have undoubtedly benefitted from linkages between policies: if we have a Single Market, we must have Economic and Monetary Union, etc. What has, however, been most impressive is the way in which once the initial breakthrough had been accomplished and the veto became an instrument of the past, all the Community institutions, and not just the Commission, demonstrated their autonomy. Member state politics, needless to say, are still very important, but in a situation in which no one member state can block, their governments have been forced to grapple with a new, virtually self-contained kind of game, involving coalition building, compromises and deals, taking the government concerned as often as not beyond the agreed national position.

The accomplishment of the greater part of the 1992 legislative program is one obvious yardstick of the new mobility in the system. It is not, however, by any means the only one. To an extent which is still only partially perceived in national capitals, power has been wrested not only from Parliaments, but also from individual state governments. At a recent meeting in Brussels, Dr. Werner of Daimler Benz observed that the bottom line on any conversation with the Bonn Minister of Environment was, inevitably, that however much he might sympathize with the position of German industry, his government's views were subject to agreement in Brussels. The exponential growth of corporate offices in Brussels in the past two or three years, including the Daimler Benz office itself, provides visible proof of the new political reality. Looking forward into the new decade, it seems increasingly probable that the Community will evolve toward an established European Union or Federation with a written constitution which spells out more systematically and comprehensively the roles and rights of the various institutions and the all-important relationships between Community-level government and government in the member states and the regions. This Final Act will probably not materialize, however, until toward the end of the decade. Before then, we will go through an intermediate process which, in the manner of the Single European Act itself, will combine legitimization of advances made since the Act—the *de facto* extension of majority voting to a great deal of Community business not covered by the Act, and the increasing integration of European Political Cooperation with the external policies of the communities—with a program for further development under most of the principal headings of Community business, more particularly Economic and Monetary Union, foreign policy and the roles of the institutions.

As far as the *Economic and Monetary Union* component of the next phase of negotiations is concerned, the Community is now firmly committed to start negotiations in December 1990. A considerable body of work has been done, first in the Delors Committee and then subsequently in the Guigou Committee, the European Commission and elsewhere on both the terms of reference of the negotiations and the principal characteristics of an eventual agreement. In assessing the prospects of these negotiations, it is important once again to emphasize how far the Community has already advanced toward the goal which the negotiators will doubtless define more clearly and make more binding. The Delors Committee report on Economic and Monetary Union established three necessary conditions for a monetary union:

- the assurance of total and irreversible convertibility of currencies;
- complete liberalization of capital transactions and full integration of banking and other financial markets; and
- the elimination of margins of fluctuation and the irrevocable locking of exchange rate parities.

The first two conditions have already been met by the first half of 1990 by almost all member states. As to the third, 11 years of the European Monetary System have led to a situation in which seven of the EC Twelve have drastically reduced, if not abandoned, the use of exchange rate policy vis-á-vis each other as an instrument of domestic economic management, an eighth (Italy) has made a serious effort in the last few months to join the inner club, and a ninth (Spain) is committed to doing so. The other three countries, Greece, Portugal, and the United Kingdom are still "outside," though all three are party to the management of the system through the normal institutions of the European Community, and in particular the Monetary Committee, the Central Bank Governors and the ECOFIN (Economic and Finance Ministers' Council). They are also committed with the others to begin "phase 1" of the Delors' Plan on July 1, 1990. This means amongst other things that sterling should in principle join the Exchange Rate Mechanism sometime fairly soon thereafter. The timing of Greek and Portuguese participation is more open, but also less significant. Agreement to special regimes in both cases would hardly constitute a serious blow to the establishment of the monetary side of the Union.

On the *economic* side too, a great deal is already in place. The Delors Committee identified four basic elements of an economic union:

- a single Market within which persons, goods, services and capital can move freely;
- competition policy and other measures aimed at strengthening market mechanisms;
- common policies aimed at structural change and regional development;
- macroeconomic policy coordination, including binding rules for budgetary policies.

Of the four, only the last represents a serious problem, and even here one should not ignore the considerable degree of macroeconomic policy coordination that has already developed without binding rules, as a result of the operation of the EMS and the management of Community affairs in general. Peer pressure, not to mention on occasions outright hegemony by the strongest member of the group during the last 12 years, have resulted in a conspicuous convergence of economic fundamentals. It is not even clear that for a functioning economic and monetary union binding budgetary rules will be necessary, but even if they are deemed to be so, the Community already has a strong springboard.

All this is not intended to imply that the negotiations which will begin in December 1990 will be trouble-free. They should not, however, be particularly troublesome. Recent suggestions therefore that they might be completed within six months are by no means far fetched. If they are, we could achieve a timetable for full Economic and Monetary Union along the lines of the following plan, shown in Table 4.1, developed by my colleagues Daniel Gros and Niels Thygesen in a recent CEPS Paper.

It is always possible that there may as on other occasions in the last 40 years be trouble with the British. In the light of political developments within the United Kingdom over the past year, however, this cannot be taken for granted. On the contrary, it is not at all improbable that the British will catch up with the rest even on a fast track like the one described by Gros and Thygesen. If for some reason or other they cannot, it is virtually inconceivable that they would try to block their partners—and still less conceivable that their partners would accept their veto if they tried. The likeliest result of continuing British skepticism would be yet another "transitional" regime, which would be a nuisance to everybody, humiliating to the British, but scarcely a disaster for the Community.

The path to EMU would seem therefore to be a relatively straightforward one. Rather larger questions marks hang over the EPU negotiations which will deal with the political and institutional issues involved in creating a *European Political Union*, or perhaps still better a European Union. As a result not least of the collapse of the Berlin Wall and all that has happened since, it now seems more than likely that the European Council, the supreme

Table 4.1 Tentative Scenario for EC Agenda

Institutional legal	Monetary policy, EMS, EMU	Individual Country Adjustment
1990 Stage I starts	Italy goes to ±2.25% margin: full capital mobility within EC8—UK	
1991 Intergovernmental Conference agrees on EMU Treaty	UK joins EMS with ±2.25% margin: Spain goes to ±2.25% margin	Budgetary and external imbalances in Spain, Italy, Greece and Portugal reduced
1992 EMU Treat ratified by EC12 (+ Austria and Norway)	Full capital mobility within EC10 + Austria and Norway	
1993 Stage II starts, ESCB created (by EC14?), special status for Greece and Portugal?	Final realignment? eduction of margins 10 ± 1% except for Greece and Portugal	
1994 Intergovernmental Conferences agrees on reform of EC institutions	Additional currencies from EFTA join stage II with margins of ± 1%	Budgetary and external imbalances in Greece and Portugal to be fully adjusted
1995 Revised Treat on EC institutions Decision to go to stage III		
1996 Stage III starts, Special status for Greece and Portugal ends.	Irrevocably-fixed rates for EC14. Preparations for common currency begin	
1998-2000 Transition to common currency for EC		

Source: Adapted from a paper by Daniel Gros and Niels Thygesen

policy-making body within the European Community, involving as it does all the heads of government and state, plus the President of the Commission, will decide in the first half of this year to include political and institutional questions in the negotiating agenda over the next two years. It is still not clear whether they will decide on a separate process from the EMU negotiations or whether they will combine the two. Whichever decision they take, however, the two will inevitably be linked, substantively if not formally.

Given the lack of any broadly agreed strategy, comparable to the three-stage plan sketched out by the Delors Committee, it would be foolish to claim any certainty about how the political negotiations will develop. There are, however, a number of clues in deadlines already known or more or less fixed. The most important is the end date. It seems hardly possible that the Community will not have agreed on some political-institutional package in advance of the next parliamentary elections which are due to take place in 1994. Well before then, however, there are two other fixed dates that have a bearing on the process: the December 31, 1992 deadline and the agreement already set out in the Single European Act to review provisions governing foreign policy cooperation five years after the Act came into force (i.e., 1992-1993). The timing of German unification and the schedule agreed with EFTA at the end of the EC negotiations with them will also tend to concentrate the minds of negotiators and hasten rather than delay conclusion of their efforts. It is therefore by no means impossible that a package of agreed revisions to the Treaty will be put together by the winter of 1991-1992, thereby paving the way for ratification and implementation by 1993.

It is possible, but rather unlikely, that this package will already constitute a draft treaty of the Union. It seems more probable that it will cover the following ground:

- an extension of voting to cover virtually all if not all Community business;
- corresponding extension of the cooperation procedures with Parliament;
- a number of measures designed to increase the political accountability of the Commission, including new procedures for the choice of the President, the abandonment of the principle of collegiality within the Commission and the introduction of a more formal hierarchy, plus a corresponding enrichment of Parliament's powers to discipline and dismiss;
- still closer integration of the external policies of the Communities with European Political Cooperation, coupled with a commitment to develop much more systematically a Community diplomatic service;

- a formal commitment to and definition of the principle of subsidarity in the development of Community institutions.

A package of this kind would already constitute a significant advance. It would not, however, of itself create a European Union in the formal sense of that term. This final stage will probably be postponed beyond 1995. If, however, the imminent negotiations on both Economic and Monetary Union and political reform sketched out above proceed according to plan, the formal constitution of a European Union toward the end of the decade will be more a rationalization of a reality virtually achieved than a bold new step into an unknown future.

If and when this Union emerges, it will by definition be quite different from existing federations in many important respect. In institutional terms, the architecture created 40 years ago will almost certainly survive. As a result of EMU, the Union will have its own Eurofed, but as previous pages suggested, even this institution will not be as brand new as its name might suggest. Important elements of it already exist.

Evolution, rather than revolution, will probably be the hallmark of the institutional architecture as a whole. The Commission will be more clearly than it is now the "government" of Europe. Parliament's role will be significantly greater, but it will still, almost certainly, have to accept as a fact a life a continuing major role for the Member States through the machinery of the Council. There has, in certain quarters, recently been energetic advocacy of a European Senate which could in due course supersede the Council machinery. Though in some long-term future, an institution of this kind might materialize, it seems much safer to assume that the Member States as such, who will continue to be responsible for raising and spending far more funds than the Union authorities, will insist on a continuing function themselves in the constitution. Parallels between France and California and Britain and Pennsylvania are premature, to put it mildly. They also underestimate the extent to which the Council machinery itself is already a constructive rather than restrictive element in the Community's politics.

As far as the powers of the Union are concerned, they seem likely to lie principally in:

- its control of a common currency and all that that implies;
- extensive regulatory powers, involving as now not only legislation but also supervision of implementation;
- increasing dominance in the external policy sphere, with the discipline over domestic policy at all levels that this almost automatically entails;
- common expenditures which, though limited in size and certainly of no general macroeconomic significance, can make a material differ-

ence in certain policy areas (e.g., research and development) and certain regions (e.g., the poorer Community countries);

- priority-setting in most if not all spheres of government, through the increasing cohesiveness of the European Council/General Affairs Council, which have already acquired and will increasingly acquire a life and logic of their own, independent of separate member states' politics;
- peer-pressure on national governments through the Council machinery reinforced by the "spillover" effect of policies for which the Community has direct legal responsibility.

In summary, there are few aspects of member states' domestic life that will not be increasingly affected by the Community. Member states will, however, remain largely responsible for the Community's taxation and spending, and a whole host of "micro" policies, including, it need hardly be said, education and social policy.

EFTA and the European Economic Space

In the light of the processes discussed in the first section, the gulf between the Community approach and the Free Trade Area strategy is clearly considerable. A still bigger set of issues emerges, however, as a result of the EC's development. Is a Free Trade Area strategy viable over time for the neighbors of a Union as large and powerful as the European Community (or the United States)?

The question has in some sense been there from the beginning. EFTA was always a defensive grouping, an effort by those who did not want to join the Six to mitigate the consequences of non-membership of a club containing some of their most important trading partners. In the very different political and economic environment of the 1950s, however, the founding members of the EFTA group—the UK, Austria, Denmark, Norway, Portugal, Sweden, and Switzerland—could still make a more or less plausible case that their club was neither second class nor doomed to lose its independence. The UK's "second place" in the North Atlantic system represented by NATO, the OECD and the Bretton Woods institutions was still undisputed, and the authority of these institutions themselves in the most important questions of economic, foreign and defence policies was hardly threatened by the decision of the member states to constitute first a coal and steel community and then a customs union. Whatever the long-term political ambitions of the Community's founders, a European Political Union was a remote dream, the practicability of which was by no means established. The methods of the EFTA club by contrast represented an application at a regional level of the larger Western Club's well-tried experience in inter-governmental, consensus-building cooperation. The list of items covered by the Stockholm convention establishing EFTA is extensive: the means by which the problems were to be resolved through a Council serviced by a small secretariat.

The subsequent history of EFTA is full of contradictions. Economic reality has more often than not been at variance with political perceptions or preoccupations.

In terms of trading patterns, EFTA states including a newer member, Finland, are fully aligned with the European Community norm. In terms of economic performance, they are all without exception, above the norm. EFTA companies like Volvo or Nestlé or the Swiss chemical multinationals or Nokia, are as successful—and as European—as most, if not all EC companies in their sectors. In a CEPS paper five years ago, Henry Ergas gave convincing evidence of a two-speed high-technology Europe with the EFTA states, Denmark, Germany, and the Netherlands, in one group and the rest of the EC, with the possible exception of Italy, as difficult as ever to classify, in the other. As European transport planners look forward to an era of high-speed trains running from north to south, fewer but better airlines, and more closely integrated road networks, the English Channel despite the Tunnel still looks a more formidable obstacle than the Baltic or the North Sea, let alone the Alps. There will be a Tunnel, it must be presumed, but fast trains will go slower between the English coast and London and stop there. The Irish, the Welsh, the Scots and everybody north of Watford will as usual pay the price of London's heavy-handed insularity.

The EFTA balance sheet is in almost every respect, therefore, very positive. Yet EFTA collectively and its member states individually have for much of the 30 years since the association was founded displayed profound anxiety. This anxiety has persisted despite a series of agreements with the EC from the 1960s onward which have in many ways been remarkably generous. Given the widespread hope amongst the original Six that Britain would eventually become a member of the Community, the Six's desire to maintain good relations with EFTA in the initial, British period were perhaps hardly surprising. This general goodwill continued, however, after the defection of the British and the Danes. The Community did not, it is true, treat the EFTA as such at this point, but the Free Trade Agreements with all EFTA members that were concluded in the early 1970s were virtually identical. They provided for complete free trade in industrial and processed agricultural products within a period of less than ten years. Primary agricultural products and fisheries were excluded. Joint committees were established to administer the agreements.

In 1984, the two sides went further. Following a joint ministerial meeting between EC and all the EFTA governments at Luxembourg on April 9, 1984, at which, to quote the final declaration, they "took stock of more than a decade of cooperation and free trade and laid down orientations to continue, deepen and extend cooperation within the framework of and beyond the

Free Trade Agreements," the ministers decided to work together to transform what was already, in their own words, "the largest system of free trade in the world within which one quarter of world trade took place" into a "dynamic European economic space."

More specifically, they agreed to tackle the new generation of trade policy questions: standards, technical barriers, border facilities, rules of origin, unfair trade practices, state aids, and access to government procurement. They also agreed to broaden and deepen cooperation in research and development, with particular emphasis being placed on industrial and technological fields of the future, "such as telecommunications, information systems and the new audiovisual media." Cooperation and consultation were to be extended too to transport, agriculture, fisheries and energy, working conditions, social protection, culture, consumer protection, the environment, tourism, and intellectual property. They would also work together in multilateral fora such as the OECD, Gatt, IMF and the World Bank.

The Luxembourg Declaration, which already anticipated the general philosophy of the Single Market program, was enforced over the following years through a plethora of joint working parties, consultative committees, etc., in which, inevitably, EFTA as such began to assume a profile distinct from its stubbornly sovereign member states. Within the Association, the Brussels ambassadors in particular began to emerge as a cohesive group pursuing, as they had to, their individual national interests within a highly developed system of consultation and cooperation. They were helped by a number of commissioners in the first Delors Commission, who while committed to the autonomy of the EC, were conspicuously well-disposed toward the EFTA countries. The External Trade Commissioner, Willy de Clercq, was one; so too was Lord Cockfield, the supremo of 1992. Cockfield's free trade instincts were reinforced by a personal liking particularly for the Nordic countries, which came out in frequent visits and speeches.

EFTA's *angst* persisted even so. Cockfield's White Paper, published in 1985 and sanctioned in the Single European Act, raised rather than lowered the temperature. The Austrians, as on previous occasions, were particularly sensitive and their ambassador to Brussels was called back at the end of 1986 to Vienna to devise a new "global" strategy, to deal with the European Community. The other EFTA states were not far behind. Every government and every parliament has now produced extensive reports on the implications for their respective countries of 1992. The business communities too were particularly active. In Austria, it was they who first denounced the new global strategy as impractical and called for a membership application. In Sweden, too, businessmen spoke in favor of what was (and to a large extent still is) considered the unthinkable: an application for membership even if it meant a break with Sweden's neutrality. The membership debate reopened in Norway, although here the Oslo élites once bitten in 1972 in a referendum in which their successful EC candidature was rejected by the people, were twice shy about espousing the cause again. Even in Switzerland and Finland, whose problems about membership were still more formidable, there was an almost universal disposition to go to the utmost short of membership. All in all the picture was greatly agitated and much confused by the winter of 1988-89.

At this point, President Delors intervened. In a speech at Strasbourg on January 17, 1989, which had an importance far beyond the EC-EFTA relationship, because it marked a clear assertion of leadership by the President of the Commission in the foreign policy field, Delors sketched out a new, two-pillar relationship, in which EFTA, by implication much more like the EC than it actually was or is, would be a privileged partner of the Community, jointly responsible with it in common institutions for the administration of the European Economic Space. Delors in effect invited the EFTA states to prepare a collective negotiating position and engage in a new, much more far-reaching round of negotiations, which could become an important element in the creation of the new European Village, an image which Delors coined as a counter to Gorbachev's celebrated European house.

The reaction to Delors' speech was rapid. Eight weeks later, at a meeting of EFTA Prime Ministers in Oslo, the governments concerned agreed to work together in a new negotiation. Pre negotiations began almost immediately afterwards and at a joint EC-EFTA ministerial meeting in December 1989, both sides gave the green light for formal negotiations in 1990. On the EFTA side, possibly unrealistically, there is considerable keenness to complete the process by the end of 1990 itself or at the very latest by early 1991.

What are the results of this exercise likely to be? In general terms, there is no doubt that the agreement when it is eventually concluded will mark a major step forward in the consolidation of the EC-EFTA block. With some, relatively minor exceptions, the EFTA states would seem to be ready to accept into their statute books all Community decisions governing the four freedoms of capital, goods, persons, and services since the Community was created. They have also agreed that negotiations should cover "flanking policies," such as Competition policy, environmental policy, structural funds, and social charter. There will be certain major exclusions: agriculture is one example, the approximation of indirect tax structures another. There are also some major open questions, including for example the treatment of goods and services from outside the EES, since a common frontier is of course one of the most obvious distinguishing features of the Customs Union as opposed to a free trade area. Serious though these issues are, however, there would seem to be a general optimism amongst negotiators on both sides, that ways and means can be found of settling all or most of them.

The crucial problems, however, concern legal and institutional arrangements. The assumption behind President Delors offer, and behind the negotiations as a whole was that an institutional arrangement can be established which guarantees EFTA's continuing existence as EFTA, linked but not subordinate to the European Community. There are, however, at least two fundamental question marks against this assumption. In the first place, are the EFTA member states themselves prepared to concede to EFTA institutions the kind of supranational powers which would almost certainly be necessary if there is to be anything approaching joint decision making between the EC and EFTA? The EFTA states' increasing concern with the power of the Community has forged a much greater solidarity amongst them than they had previously, and they are now used to functioning as a group on an increasingly wide range of issues. They remain, however, an Association of states and there is very little evidence to suggest that some of the more important of them, notably the Swiss, would be prepared to contemplate anything like the Community's majority voting amongst themselves. The second question is still more fundamental. Would the community in reality be ready to make its own final decision contingent on agreement with EFTA? The answer is quite clearly negative.

The regime that emerges, therefore, seems unlikely to be totally satisfying from an EFTA standpoint. EFTA states will have to accept that in the final analysis it is the Community that decides. What they can hope for—and should obtain—is a more transparent and reliable set of procedures ensuring that the EFTA position is known and taken seriously before the Community decides: decision-*shaping* rather than decision-*making*, to use the current jargon. It is also highly probable that the Community may be open to far reaching cooption and cooperation in the all important functions of implementation and control. EFTA judges may well, for example, sit with European Community judges when EFTA cases are heard in the European Court of Justice. Similarly, the well-established practice of delegation of implementation and control functions to national administrations within the Community can easily be extended to countries whose administrations are as advanced as those of EFTA.

For at least some EFTA states, an agreement along the lines sketched out above will almost certainly be satisfactory, at any rate in the short-term. For Finland and Switzerland, for example, the difficulties in the way of membership of the EC are so fundamental that even a less-than-perfect arrangement which nevertheless enhances their relationship with the Community is better than the existing situation. This view will not, however, be universally held in EFTA. It is already clear that Austria regards membership as the only realistic option. Others may follow suit, including some whose neutrality is of a different character from those of either Switzerland or Finland (or for that matter Austria).

To the countries concerned—and, it must be admitted for many within the Community—it seems self-evident that if and when these new candidates apply, they should, after due negotiation, be admitted. Article 237 of the Treaty of Rome specifically states that any European state (by implication democratic in character) may apply. Would it not therefore be highly inconsistent for the Community to reject these newcomers, or indeed several others who may in the course of a few years want to join?

The reasoning is simple and attractive. On closer examination, however, the policy of open arms toward EFTA—the final act of reconciliation with the prodigal son more than 30 years after the break in the family—looks far more problematic and even dangerous. The EC-EFTA relationship which until now could be pursued inside the comfort and stability of Western Europe alone must now be thought through afresh in the context of a pan-European structure embracing not only the smaller states of Eastern Europe but also the Soviet Union.

The EC, EFTA, and the New Europe

The issues involved in the economic and political reconstruction of post-Communist Europe are so complex, and the uncertainties so numerous that it is far too early to predict what will happen. It is not too early, however, to try to assess what should happen. On the contrary, there is a very real danger that the new European architecture may be fundamentally flawed because the principles on which it is built have been inadequately thought through. No part of Europe can be insulated from the future consequences of poor design in any part. The EC-EFTA relationship is manifestly of concern to all: it must, however, itself be reviewed in the light of its relevance to the overall structure.

The analysis offered in subsequent pages is based on certain assumptions which ought to be spelled out at the beginning.

- The collapse of Communism must in large measure be seen as a victory for market economics. It is essential therefore that the new political architecture of Europe should guarantee both the Soviet Union and the recently liberated Eastern European states the best possible framework for free economies to develop and flourish. This means the minimum of restrictions: a Europe without frontiers from the Atlantic to the Urals, with freedom of movement of goods, capital, services, and persons.

- The changes in the East do not, however, mean that Europe is no longer burdened with a security problem. Perpetual peace cannot be taken for granted on a continent in which there are still very formidable concentrations of armed forces and military hardware, including nuclear weapons, where ethnic fault lines—notably in Eastern Europe and the Soviet Union—are a constant reminder of previous instability and potential unrest, and where Europe's frontiers touch at so many points on the Islamic World, which for reasons as diverse as theology and demography seems certain to pose problems to Europeans in both East and West.

- Within the New Europe, the Soviet Union or its successor, will remain in almost every respect a major power, qualitatively in another league in several important ways from any other European state. This has two important consequences. In the first place, any durable pan-European order must be built on the assumption that the Soviet Union or Russia is part of it. Second, given the continuing military dimension in relations between East and West in Europe, Soviet strength even if it is deprived of the Warsaw Pact must be balanced in one way or another in the West.

- Although it must be presumed that US administrations will continue to recognize their profound interest in European security, and therefore their need to be associated with its maintenance, it seems highly unlikely that the US presence and role in Europe over the coming years will remain at levels comparable to those maintained throughout the post-War period. Furthermore, the chances of political semi-isolationism must be all the greater as the Western Europeans themselves do not shoulder a greater part of their own security costs, both in terms of men and money.

- A united Germany within an integrated European structure can only over time be of still great benefit in economic terms to the European Community and Europe as a whole: a united Germany which in one way or another slipped outside the integrated structure would be a fresh and dangerous source of instability.

- The momentum toward European political integration within the European Community is such, for reasons discussed at length in the beginning of this paper, that its achievement can now be assumed as a realistic working hypothesis in any discussions of the future European political order. Two extremely important supplementary considerations must, however, be borne in mind. Both concern the optimal size of the European political community.

The first is its governability. The European Community has already moved from EC-6 to EC-12 and seems likely over the next year to increase, with the absorption of East Germany, to EC-12-half. It is obvious, therefore, that there is no fixed frontier and that theoretically the EC could, as many advocate, extend its membership to 24 or 25. It must, however, be doubted whether an EC of this size, with such large cultural and economic diversity, could be efficiently governed without a much larger central authority than the current European Community has or is likely to need even when it matures into a political union. The response might be: in that case let it relapse into a loose Free Trade Area or an extended European Economic Space. At least two comments are appropriate on this. In the first case a journey back toward a Free Trade Area would require the scrapping of much of the *acquis communautaires*. This is neither politically feasible nor politically desirable. For better or for worse—and in the present author's view undoubtedly for better—the strategic decision was made in the 1950s to pursue the supranational route toward political union. This step, once taken, had, as previous sections have shown, a certain inexorable logic, and it is barely conceivable that there would be any gain whatsoever from turning the clock back 40 years.

This point is emphasized by a second consideration. A European Community, loosened into a European Free Trade Area in order to accommodate a medley of newcomers, could not at the same time assume any of the key functions in relation to the Soviet Union, the US and Germany, which, as previous paragraphs have implied, it is ideally placed to perform.

Objections to a Community of 24 do not, however, stem only from its potential ungovernability. Even if we assumed that this difficulty was overcome, and EC-24 was as strong and efficient as EC-12 is clearly in the process of becoming, we would be faced with a danger of an altogether different kind. An effective European Union of 24 or 25, stretching from the Atlantic to the Western frontiers of Russia or the Soviet Union could over time be seen as a threat by the latter and therefore as a source of major destabilization in the next century. If European history teaches us one thing, it is that the rulers of Russia, the Soviet Union, or Novgorod do not like continental powers stretching from the Atlantic coast to or within their frontiers. There are therefore strong grounds for arguing that in the interests of both the Community and Europe, the EC should remain at more or less its present size.

Where then do these general considerations lead in the quest for a balanced European architecture? They lead first to yet another maxim: in the general reconstruction of Europe, politics must take primacy over economics. This does not mean that the first principle outlined above should be ignored: it simply means that it must be balanced by the overriding requirement to ensure that the political design is sound.

We begin therefore with the political order. The key players whose position on the board have to be clearly defined are Russia or the Soviet Union, the EC, Germany and the US. There must, of course, in addition be a general European political architecture, evolving presumably from the CSCE process, in which all European nations (plus the US and Canada) would be involved, but there is no way in which this organization can or should become a substitute for clearly defined relations between the major actors.

In this perspective, the best possible structure would be one based on a strong Soviet Union or Russia, on EC-12 including the United Germany and having the full responsibilities of a European Union, including in due course military responsibilities, allied with the US in a reorganized NATO. The key variable in this is of course the EC. Because the European Community does not yet have a defense capability—and for other less worthy reasons—some of the existing medium-sized players, notably France and the UK, have displayed a strong interest in a continuing separation between defence and economic policy, of a kind which the Western Alliance tolerated since the war, largely, however, because the knot was tied in Washington by US leadership. If would be highly undesirable if this division were to persist. Economic policy is as much a part of security policy as the capacity to strike back. Security policy includes not only the maintenance of an economy capable of fighting, it embraces still more importantly active policies of economic aid, advice, and cooperation. These latter are already the responsibility of the European Community institutions and as the European Community institutions mature into political union, it seems only logical that they should acquire a full range of security responsibilities. In practical terms, the obvious context within which to develop this kind of scenario is not only the EC's internal discussion, but the current, expanding EC-US dialogue called for by President Bush and James Baker.

Where, in political terms, does this leave the other players? As has already been indicated, it is essential that they should be associated with a stronger pan-European organization, based presumably on the CSCE process. This would be the governing body of Gorbachev's European house or Delors' European village. It is perfectly conceivable, however, that for economic reasons (see below) some of the other participating nations should form small sub-groups. It is to be hoped, however, that the principal, if not the exclusive role of the smaller confederations or unions would be non-military. Acceptance of the need for clearly defined relations between the big players is one thing; the resurgence of lesser players' fully equipped in military terms quite another. There is no need to return to a multipolar system of the kind that Europe had in the 19th century.

As far as the economic side of the picture is concerned, the political structure outlined in previous paragraphs need not in any way prevent the continuing development of market economies and the maximization of free trade. A simplification of the security structure does not necessarily imply the emergence of two European fortresses, one in Russia and the other in EC-12 (or 14). On the contrary, the structure will only be stable if the two major European powers are not fortresses in economic terms. We seek a Europe without frontiers.

This of course implies a pan-European institutional framework. The CSCE process might yet again prove to be a useful base: the recent meeting in Bonn was moderately encouraging in this respect. Another European institution too has a role to play, namely the Council of Europe with its commitment to the maintenance of human rights and the encouragement of cultural exchanges, etc. Both institutions must be given a major boost in the near future. It would be naive, however, to ignore a fundamental characteristic of the current European political economy which is likely to remain valid for a very long time to come. This is, quite simply, that the EC is economically in a different league from every other European player, including the Soviet Union. General political architecture must therefore be developed so that it does not impede the development of a complex pattern of bilateral relationships revolving around the EC in terms of currency—an ecu zone—trade, and technological or managerial know-how. The EC seems bound to be the rule setter and pace setter for the continent as a whole. That is why, amongst other things, the extended EC-EFTA dialogue has such important long-term implications. EFTA, as we have suggested above, will have to settle for less than a whole loaf. If, however, as seems likely, the EFTA-EC negotiations obliged the Community to give EFTA a real place in the decision shaping and an acknowledged role in the implementation and control of Community legislation, this could become a factor of major consequence for the European structure as a whole.

There is one other very important dimension. If the architecture discussed above is to be secured in the long term, it must itself be integrated into the global architecture. The emergence of an EC hegemon in economic terms which is already a partial reality, will create challenges in the management of the global economy as a whole. It goes without saying that structural changes will have to be made in groups such as the G7.

The implications of the changes sketched out in previous paragraphs extend, however, far further than mere fiddling with seats at an international table. We are moving towards a world order based on regional blocks or zones. As I have argued in several places already, it does not seem to me that this is a threatening development. On the contrary, it provides grounds for hope rather than despair. It will, however, require a great deal of thought and skilful negotiation if the transition is to be comfortably accomplished.

5

The Realities of a
North American
Economic Alliance

Gary C. Hufbauer
Jeffrey J. Schott

Introduction

The announcement that the United States and Mexico may soon begin negotiations on a free trade agreement (FTA) breathes political life into the idea of a North American economic alliance. Coming on the heels of the US-Canada Free Trade Agreement (ratified in 1989), the US-Mexico trade and investment pact (signed October 1989), and the recent Canada-Mexico framework agreement (signed March 1990), the implications of prospective US-Mexico talks are significant, although their prospects should not be exaggerated.

A US-Mexico FTA would not presage a unified North American market, accomplishing the same degree of deep integration now underway in the European Community. It would not deal with labor mobility or monetary union; indeed, the bare mention of these topics could block even the launch of US-Mexico talks. Nor would it lead to completely free merchandise trade in the 1990s. Rather, an FTA would gradually phase out tariffs on a continental basis, but, for the time being, leave many quotas and other nontariff barriers subject to piecemeal removal. In this respect, the parallel with the deliberate pace of integration in the European Community in the 1960s is appropriate.

To be sure, a North American economic alliance has enormous economic and political appeal. Leaving aside the depth and timetable of economic integration—the specifics of the economic alliance—unification of the American, Canadian, and Mexican economies would yield a market as large and populous as the European Community (EC) and European Free Trade Association (EFTA) combined. Here is the profile for 1988:

	GNP	*Population*
EC plus EFTA	$5,385 billion	357 million
North America	$5,528 billion	355 million

Source: IMF, *International Financial Statistics*, February 1990

To the casual observer, numbers such as these suggest that the combination of American capital and technology, Canadian resources, and Mexican labor would create an economic powerhouse.

But it is worth stepping back from size comparisons to ask what each party to a North American economic alliance would gain. Over a period of years, a North American alliance could significantly boost Mexico's GNP and two-way trade since, in economic terms, Mexico is the smallest, most protected, and poorest of the three nations. But what would the United States and Canada gain from extending their relationship to include Mexico? Cold arithmetic suggests that the addition of Mexico to the US-Canada Free Trade Area would exert little impact on American or Canadian GNP or exports, since Mexico is small relative to its partners (3.2% of North American GNP; 4.5% of total exports). Moreover, a North American economic alliance is tangential to the core international economic concerns of each of the three partners:

- With the end of the Cold War, the United States is girding itself for an economic race, with high technology the grand prize. A North American economic alliance including Mexico would play, at best, a marginal role in this race. The key relations—both as competitors and partners—are with Japan and the European Community.

- Mexico's short-term problems are external debt and monetary stability. A North American alliance would help solve these problems by enhancing the Mexican investment atmosphere, but the contribution might not be decisive over the next few years.

- Canada is faced with a troubled federal system. The demise of the Meech Lake Accord in June 1990 seems to portend a weaker federal government, and stronger provincial governments. In this setting, the key issue for the federal government is to retain its dominance over Canada's external commercial policy. If anything, a North American economic alliance could add to the centrifugal tendencies in the Canadian system.

Taken together, these core concerns suggest that a North American economic alliance can not be the centerpiece of commercial diplomacy in any of the three nations. On the other hand, a North American economic alliance would help allay two central concerns in the US-Mexico relationship: whether Mexico will eventually recover the financial stability to service its external debt; and whether Mexican economic growth can stem the tide of immigration to the north. In addition, the formation of a North American economic alliance would convey powerful political signals:

- for the United States: a decision to counter the growing power of the European Community and Japan with its "own" regional trading arrangement;
- for Mexico: a decision to abandon definitively its historic aversion to sharing economic sovereignty with its northern neighbor;
- for Canada: a willingness to enlarge the special Ottawa-Washington relationship to include Mexico City.

The implementation of the US-Canada Free Trade Agreement, and the recent conclusion of US-Mexico and Canada-Mexico framework agreements on trade and investment, provide institutional underpinnings for a prospective North American economic community. Moreover, the economics of a North American alliance has anticipated the politics, making the task of further negotiations somewhat easier. Both Canada and Mexico conduct about two-thirds of their trade with the United States, and each hosts substantial US direct investment. Although the preponderance of foreign investment in the United States originates in Europe and Japan, the United States benefits from substantial Canadian direct investment, and hosts large sums of Mexican portfolio and real estate investment (often labeled flight capital). US trade is also far more diversified than that of its neighbors (about one-quarter each to Canada-Mexico and the EC, and about one-third to East Asia).

All in all, the economic attractions are sufficiently strong, and the institutional framework sufficiently advanced, that a coherent North American economic alliance seems an odds-on favorite by the year 2000. The interesting questions fall into two groups. First, what are the likely goals of the alliance and what is the path to reach these goals? Second, what are the consequences of a North American alliance for the GATT system and world trade relations? Most of this paper is devoted to the first set of questions; at the end we briefly speculate on the systemwide consequences of a North American economic alliance.

The Goal and Paths to North American Economic Integration

Two distinct goals can be identified for a North American economic alliance: a "high goal," expressed by the ambitious title North American Economic Community (NAEC), and a "low goal," captured by the more modest title North American Free Trade Area (NAFTA). Further, there are two distinct paths to the ultimate goal: a "high road," in which a grand leap is made over two to four years, and a "low road," travelled step-by-step over a longer period.

Our thesis is that North American economic integration will come closer to resembling NAFTA than NAEC, and that it will be reached step-by-step, rather than in a grand leap.

North American Economic Community: Mission Improbable

As Europe has demonstrated, the phrase "economic community" holds the promise of ultimately achieving the four grand symbols of economic integration: internal free trade, monetary union, labor mobility, and comparable social rights throughout the region. Unlike the situation in Europe, prospects for economic integration within the North American region face several distinct hurdles:

- The main problem is US dominance. The GNP of the United States is more than 85% of the combined regional total, and the population of the United States is nearly 70% of the total. In practical terms, Canada and Mexico would need to adapt their economic institutions to existing US models, rather than participate in the design of new institutions through the process of give and take that characterized European integration in the 1960s and 1970s. (At that time, there were five roughly balanced states in the European Community: Germany, France, Italy, Benelux—viewed as a single entity—and the United Kingdom.) Unlike the nations that have more recently joined the EC (Greece, Spain, and Portugal) or now want to join (Austria and Hungary), neither Canada nor Mexico is prepared to restructure its fundamental economic institutions to match those of the United States.

- The second problem is the large disparity in per capita income between Mexico and its northern neighbors. The larger the income disparity between prospective Community members, the harder the process of economic integration. The EC spanned a wide divide when it incorporated Spain and Portugal, countries whose per capita GNP levels at the time of accession (January 1987) were $6,010 and $2,830, or 51 and 24% of average EC-10 per capita GNP, respectively. By comparison, Mexico's per capita GNP is only one-tenth that of the United States, and one-eighth that of Canada.

- The third problem, related to the second, is labor absorption: there were fewer people to accommodate at the lower income levels in the EC case, thus limiting the adjustment burden—or simplifying the task of paying for adjustment assistance. The combined population of Spain and Portugal is 18% of the EC-10 total, compared to Mexico whose population is almost one-third the combined size of the United States and Canada.

These three large obstacles to a North American Economic Community are compounded by a range of smaller difficulties. The Europe 1992 process demonstrates that meaningful economic integration requires an end to member state industrial subsidies, barriers created by product standards, different trucking requirements, wide differences in VAT and excise taxes, capital controls, differences in competition policy, etc. (Hufbauer, 1990). Just listing these hurdles suggests that economic union in North America is well out of reach until the 21st century. In the meantime, less sweeping integration must set the stage for serious exploration of the implications of a true economic community.

North American Free Trade Area: The Outer Limit

Even the goal of a North American Free Trade Area (NAFTA), for all its economic appeal, quickly runs into hard political limits. Many labor-intensive industries in the United States could be exposed to blistering competition from Mexico: textiles and apparel, ceramics, leather goods, fruits and vegetables, and a range of assembled products. At the same time, many long-protected Mexican industries would face unfettered foreign competition for the first time ever: automobiles, household appliances, pharmaceuticals, machinery, wheat and corn.

Considering the difficulties of navigating the US-Canada FTA through Washington and Ottawa, far greater domestic obstacles can be anticipated to a NAFTA. To illustrate the difficulties that lie ahead, it is worth pondering the Caribbean Basin Initiative. Despite the exceedingly small size of the Caribbean nations, and the large US political stakes in a stable Caribbean area, it proved impossible to eliminate US barriers against merchandise items of immediate export interest to the CBI nations—sugar, textiles and apparel, footwear, etc.

In addition, the United States, Mexico, and Canada must be concerned about the fallout of NAFTA talks both for the Uruguay Round and the longer-term evolution of the world trading system. Although proposals for a US-Mexico FTA or a broader NAFTA may be intended to energize the

Uruguay Round, the FTA prod may actually distract the focus of other countries from the GATT talks by signalling that access to the US market is best achieved through bilateral negotiations. Over the longer term, serious NAFTA talks will almost certainly prompt Japan to forge stronger bilateral ties with China, other Asian nations, and Oceania, and the European Community will see justification in pursuing the path it already prefers— concentrating on strengthening European trade ties ahead of global trade ties.

"High Road" or "Low Road"?

A "high road" for NAFTA would entail intense negotiations over a period of two to four years. These negotiations would produce a road map for the complete elimination of border barriers. Most tariffs and non-tariff barriers would be phased out over five to ten years; the most sensitive sectors would be entitled to slower elimination of their border barriers over ten years or longer; but very few sectors would be exempt from liberalization.

In our view, the high road is not plausible. The prospective economic shocks in all three countries generated by the removal of all nontariff barriers would be too great, even with liberal phasing; correspondingly, the counterwave of political resistance would be huge. A better model, we suggest, is provided by the evolution of economic relations between Australia and New Zealand.

For many decades, Australia and New Zealand were the most protectionist countries in the OECD area with respect to manufactured goods. They protected their markets not only against European, American, and Japanese manufactures, but also against each other. Since the early 1960s, however, Australia and New Zealand have implemented two major agreements that dramatically liberalized trans-Tasmanian trade. The New Zealand-Australia Free Trade Agreement, which operated for 16 years from 1966 to 1982, reduced tariff barriers across a limited range of products. The far more extensive Australia-New Zealand Closer Economic Relations Agreement, which did not take effect until January 1983, covered all goods unless specifically excepted, and a wide range of services. It dismantled protective barriers according to a prearranged timetable.

In August 1988, responding to a favorable political climate, the two prime ministers signed several protocols to expand the CER to cover additional sectors such as finance, transportation, and the freedom of labor movement between the two countries. Both nations agreed upon the gradual and automatic removal of all frontier barriers to trade in manufactured and agricultural goods by July 1990, five years ahead of the original timetable.

The lesson for North America from the Tasmanian Basin is straightforward: better to sketch the goal in the broadest strokes, and then fill in the details step-by-step as political opportunity permits, than to announce a grand plan at the outset, and generate a backlash of political opposition.

Interests of the Partners

Mexico, Canada, and the United States each has its own reasons for pursuing a North American Free Trade Area. The reasons are quite different; the degree of complementarity will largely determine the scope and pace of talks.

Mexico

As the smallest and most protected economy, Mexico has the most to gain over time from a North American Free Trade Area. Such an agreement would reinforce and accelerate the pace of domestic reforms currently being implemented, and would guarantee access to the broader North American market.

Of the three nations, Mexico thus can most easily be cast in the classic role of *demandeur*. As *demandeur*, Mexico must be prepared to make most of the "concessions," that is, most of the reforms in its own economy.

Before pursuing new reforms under NAFTA, Mexico will need to deal with the immediate problem of financing its economic growth. Servicing the foreign debt will remain an ever-present burden (despite the stretch out negotiated under the Brady Plan); financing of the current account deficit remains tenuous and dependent on new lending from the international financial institutions, repatriation of flight capital ($2.5-3.0 billion in 1989) (*Financial Times*, 1990), and new foreign direct investment. In addition, Salinas must halt the alarming increase in inflation which—if not controlled quickly—could disrupt his entire, and largely successful, economic stabilization program (Gurria, 1990: A13).

The Mexican strategy under Salinas has been to encourage import competition to help dampen inflation, and to finance the resulting trade deficits with foreign direct investment and new lending. In the past year, Salinas has taken a series of steps to improve the climate for foreign investors in Mexico. A quick review of those measures may be useful.

Import Liberalization. Since 1985, Mexico has substantially reformed its trade regime (Trigueros, 1989). In incremental steps, it has reduced tariffs significantly, harmonized its tariff structure, abolished official prices, and removed most import licensing requirements.

The program of import liberalization has recently been extended to the computer and pharmaceutical sectors. In March 1990, Mexico eliminated licensing restrictions on computer imports and announced a three-year duty exemption for imported components—conditioned on the firm's domestic value-added—to stimulate domestic production. At the same time, the Mexican Commerce Ministry abolished the requirement for prior import permits for 46 of 80 pharmaceutical inputs, with the remainder to be liberalized by 1993 (Johns, 1990: 9).

Privatization. The Salinas government has embarked on an extensive privatization program. By the end of 1989, about 650 parastatals had been dismantled, consolidated, or sold. Of the 210 companies that have been sold, Mexican groups bought 91% and 9% were bought by foreigners or joint ventures. At their peak, parastatals accounted for 16% of Mexico's GDP; by January 1990, this ratio had been trimmed to 13% (including PEMEX). (Rogozinski, 1990). The sale of PEMEX would raise concerns even more explosive than those voiced during the Canadian debate over the energy provisions of the US-Canada FTA.

Most recently, President Salinas announced plans in May 1990 to denationalize the banking sector. Legislative authorization for this reform was quickly attained.

While most of the companies dismantled to date have been small and relatively unknown, the privatization program has also reached several of the "crown jewels" of the parastatal domain: Mexicana Airlines, Telmex, and, most recently, the proposed sale of two large steel plants that are part of the Sidermex state steel group (Altos Hornos de Mexico or AHMSA, and Siderugica Lazaro Cardenas-Las Truchas or Sicartsa). Among the parastatals, AHMSA ranks third in size behind PEMEX and Telmex (Johns, 1990: 6). These high-profile sales have been defended as a way to get the government out from expending large sums to cover operating losses and large capital investments, and thus free up resources for social welfare programs. The sale of Telmex is the most ambitious venture to date; foreigners will be allowed to purchase 49% of the company when shares are floated (*Financial Times*, 1990: 6).

The Mexican government has pursued a mixture of deregulatory and privatization policies to spur the competitiveness of Mexican industry. The deregulation policy has had its biggest impact so far in the transport sector, where reforms reportedly led to 30 percent cost savings in 1989 (*Financial Times*, 1990: 6). In the civil aviation sector, privatization of Aeromexico and Mexicana was designed in part to promote new investment in companies facing increased competition—which in turn resulted from a new US-Mexico aviation agreement signed in 1988.

Intellectual Property Rights. As a complement to the foreign investment decree issued in May 1989, the Mexican government announced plans in January 1990 to extend patent protection for 20 years, and to revise regulations regarding technology transfer to remove some disincentives (e.g., the ten-year limit on confidentiality and contracts in technology transfer), and to limit government interference in screening such transfers to Mexico.

Pursuit of an FTA with the United States. Because of the sharp deterioration in Mexico's current account in the last quarter of 1989, Salinas has sought to further encourage foreign capital inflows by suggesting the negotiation of a US-Mexico FTA. Such an agreement would assure access to the North American market and increase competition within the Mexican market—which in turn would accelerate the ongoing reform process, and help sweep away the vestiges of statism.

Canada

Canada has several reasons to embrace a Canadian-Mexican arrangement as its contribution toward a larger North American Free Trade Area, but they are not the hard-edged economic reasons that dominate debate in Mexico City.

- One reason, with broad popular appeal, is to show Canadian concern for less-developed nations.

- A second reason is to maintain Ottawa's position as a player in the dialogue between Mexico City and Washington on immediate questions such as trade in automobiles and parts, and longer-range questions such as natural gas flows.

- The third reason is that issues will certainly arise where Mexico City and Ottawa will find common commercial interests juxtaposed against Washington. In these cases, two coordinated voices may well have more impact than two distinct voices.

The ten bilateral accords signed in March 1990 by Canada and Mexico are strongest in the non-economic subject arena. The economic framework agreement was long on hopes and aspirations—more trade and investment flows—and short on specifics. The nine non-economic accords dealt more concretely with drug trafficking, extradition, exchange of tax information, protection of the environment, agriculture, forestry, tourism, culture, and customs procedures. In a companion move, Prime Minister Mulroney indicated that Canada would at long last join the Organization of American States, thereby providing some balance against the United States and possibly reviving what has become a somnolent debating society (*Financial Times*, 1990: 6).

Although the momentum of events may require Canada to play down the costs of a broader North American economic alliance, these costs deserve academic notice.

Short-term Trade Diversion. The US-Canada Free Trade Agreement had some trade diversion consequences for Mexico. According to one set of estimates, the gross trade diversion, in terms of 1988 trade flows, was $662 million, of which $421 million was in the automotive sector and $102 million was in consumer electronics. Offsetting the diversion was $257 million of trade creation, of which the largest component was $123 million for knitting mills (Ministry of Industry and Trade, 1990). Obviously a US-Mexico agreement would work in the converse direction—diverting some trade from Canada. Autos would be most impacted in the short term, probably followed by textiles and apparel.

Long-term Trade Impact. Of far greater quantitative importance than the immediate trade diversion is the long-run trade impact, as Mexico specializes in the products of its comparative advantage. The potential disruption to both the United States and Canada of an 80 million strong low-wage country working its way up the product chain are enormous.

Over a decade, a true free trade area could lead to the wholesale contraction of certain labor-intensive industries in both the United States and Canada, for example, textiles and apparel, footwear, and ceramics. In addition, there would be a significant impact on other machine-driven industries such as automobile assembly, household appliances, and consumer electronics.

Canada, like the United States, would gain from reciprocal exports of more sophisticated products. But an FTA would certainly accelerate the restructuring of both economies out of industries that have long enjoyed protection from low-wage developing countries.

Orientation of Commercial Diplomacy. For a country of its economic size, Canada has played a uniquely strong role in the GATT and other multilateral institutions. Canada has traditionally been a leader in GATT talks, a member of the G-7, and a strong voice in the World Bank, the IMF and the OECD. On economic issues, Canada does not automatically line up with the United States, and its independence has added to Canadian credibility in world debates. A key question is whether, as part of NAFTA, Canada can keep its uniquely Canadian voice—particularly in future world discussion of such issues as mutual recognition of high-tech standards, competition policy, and research consortia.

United States

Seen from the US perspective, the consequences of a NAFTA are smallest in the economic dimension (though not insignificant) and largest in the political dimension.

In essence, a NAFTA would entail only a modest increment to the US economy, adding a US-Mexico FTA on top of the US-Canada pact. Overall, the welfare gains for the United States from trade liberalization with Mexico—a country only 1/20th its economic size—would not be significant. However, a FTA would promote economic growth in its populous neighbor, and thus help deal with the immigration problem. The United States would also benefit if the success of Mexico's open trade policy becomes a model for other democracies in the hemisphere.

In addition, the United States hopes to use the prospect of a FTA with Mexico as a prod to get developing countries to move more quickly in the Uruguay Round, much as it used the US-Canada FTA to help enlist EC and Japanese support to launch the Uruguay Round. Unlike the US-Canada FTA, however, the prospect of a NAFTA is more likely to distract the focus of developing countries from GATT talks than to encourage their pursuit of multilateral agreements.

Depending on the outcome of the Uruguay Round, these countries might find an FTA option—entailing links with either the European Community, or North America, or even Japan—a more attractive route to assure market access than the negotiation of multilateral accords in the GATT. This outcome would contribute further to the erosion of the multilateral trading system.

Agenda for a North American Free Trade Area

Both internal and external factors are propelling closer economic integration among the three countries of North America. The process is being driven by common interests in deregulation and privatization on the domestic front, by common concerns such as dealing with large current account deficits, by closer bilateral trading arrangements, and by participation in the multilateral trading system.

If the statesmen of Mexico City, Ottawa, and Washington embrace the concept of a North American Free Trade Area, it will involve a long-term, incremental process of negotiation—the "low road." Progress on the low road to closer economic integration can be made by five concrete steps:

- gradual phase-out of tariffs;
- creation of a North American automotive pact, ultimately free of production and trade distortions;
- elimination of quota restrictions on North American trade in textiles, apparel, steel, and agriculture;
- reform of Mexican investment regulations, with a special focus on energy-related investment; and
- liberalization of trade in selected services, notably finance and telecommunications.

Tariffs

The US-Canada FTA calls for the elimination of tariffs on bilateral trade by the end of 1998; this is consistent with GATT rules because the cuts are part of a broader FTA that encompasses "substantially all" of the trade between the two countries. Mexico would need to negotiate a similar arrangement with the United States and Canada, or apply the tariff cuts on a most-favored-nation basis, or face the task of obtaining a GATT waiver.

As a result of tariff liberalization instituted since 1985, Mexico's average weighted tariff is now only 6.2%, and no tariffs are higher than 20% (Salinas, 1990). Indeed, the Mexican tariff schedule is now more harmonized than that of its northern neighbors. Harmonizing a tariff schedule can be more disruptive in economic terms, and therefore a bigger step in political terms, than cutting tariffs by a linear amount. With the bigger pain out of the way for Mexico, the elimination of tariffs between the three countries of North America could be achieved by the year 2000. It might even be possible to agree on a common external tariff, by selecting the lowest rate applied by any of the three partners.

Auto Pact

Automobiles and parts are the largest component of manufactured trade between the United States and Canada (some $40.4 billion in 1988 or 31.4% of bilateral trade in manufactures), and the United States and Mexico (some $7.8 billion in 1988 or 25.9% of bilateral trade in manufactures). US–Canada trade has been regulated since 1965 by the Auto Pact, which facilitated the integration of the auto industry in the two countries.

Two recent developments should help promote the further integration of the North American auto market, and possibly lead to a trilateralization of the existing Auto Pact. The two developments are the auto provisions of the US-Canada FTA, and the implementation of the new Mexican auto decree.

While the FTA maintains the Canadian safeguards under the 1965 Auto Pact, these safeguards will become increasingly redundant as the Canadian external tariff is reduced pursuant to multilateral trade liberalization in the GATT. At the same time, the FTA will progressively eliminate the duty remission subsidies now enjoyed by Canadian producers. This step ensures a level playing field in automotive production between Canada and the United States. Incidentally, the elimination of the Canadian subsidies also will make Mexico and the United States relatively more attractive as host countries for new investment, especially by Japanese and Korean producers.

Mexico has hosted investment by the major US auto companies (as well as Volkswagen and Nissan), but has barred imports of assembled cars since the auto decree of 1962. However, in December 1989, the Mexican government issued a new auto decree that relaxes the 1962 ban on auto imports, starting in 1991, but keeps two restrictions:

- import volumes must be less than or equal to 15% of domestic sales in 1991-1992; and
- foreign exchange requirements must be balanced, producer by producer (i.e., export earnings must be greater than or equal to import costs).

In addition, the 1989 decree modified the existing local content rule, lowering the requirement that 60% of the value-added of the final product be sourced in Mexico down to 36%.

These reforms will still leave the Mexican market with a high level of protection in the 1990s. Even though Mexican automotive exports account for almost 30% of total Mexican manufactured exports (and have more than doubled since 1985), rapid growth belies the fact that "most of the Mexican production base is not currently cost competitive with the US or East Asia, due to scale and infrastructure problems" (Womack, 1989: 12). The removal of the import quotas, local content rules, and foreign exchange balancing requirements would place most Mexican assembly plants under severe competitive pressure. Yet, if liberalization is phased in gradually and foreign companies set up new plants in Mexico, the Mexican auto industry could be restructured and actually expand significantly, making it possible to lift automotive barriers within a decade and create a unified North American market.

Quotas

The hardest task will be the removal of quantitative restrictions on North American trade in textiles, apparel, steel, and agriculture. These restraints serve as a safeguard against import surges that could result from regional or multilateral tariff liberalization. Removing this safety net would expose producers in all three countries to sharp competitive pressures.

Some progress, however, has already been made in expanding quotas on textiles, apparel, and steel under the US-Mexico framework agreement. In February 1990, the United States agreed to eliminate quotas on 52 textile and apparel products and to expand quotas by an average of 25% for products that remain controlled. Mexico officials estimate that this will almost double Mexican textile and apparel exports to the United States from their 1989 level of $646 million (*International Trade Reporter*, 1990: 256-257 and *Washington Post*, 1990: H6). Agreement in GATT to unravel the Multi-Fiber Arrangement could augment this growth and possibly lead to the removal of all quotas within ten-fifteen years.

The textile agreement is patterned after the US-Mexico steel pact signed in October 1989, by which the United States doubled its annual Mexican import quota from 400,000 to 800,000 tons (*Financial Times*, 1989: 7). Looking to the future, these quotas should disappear by early 1992 under current US policies. Even if political pressures in the 1992 election year result in an extension of the steel program, it is possible to envisage quotas for Mexican steel that expand just ahead of Mexican export capabilities.

By contrast with the progress in autos, textiles and apparel, and steel, there has been little accomplished in the US-Canada or the US-Mexico context on agriculture. The US-Canada FTA negotiators came to an understanding that reforms need to be pursued in the GATT setting of multilateral trade talks rather than in the North America setting. The argument prevailed that a bigger pot of worldwide agricultural concessions, especially by the Japan and the European Community, would enable both Canada and the United States to pursue more broadbased reforms of their price support programs and other domestic subsidies. For the time being, this same logic will delay any US-Mexico or Canada-Mexico agricultural liberalization.

After the Uruguay Round, it is conceivable that the three nations could agree to standardize (if not eliminate) their price supports and other subsidies crop by crop, and to eliminate their border barriers. The greatest impact would be on Mexico: its imports of cereals would grow very significantly, and its exports of fruits, vegetables and sugar would soar.

Investment Regulations

Reforms in Mexico's foreign investment regulations announced in May 1989 bring Mexican policy much more in line with obligations set out in the US-Canada FTA. However, Mexico continues to maintain numerous performance requirements (banned by the US-Canada pact), does not commit itself to national treatment, and exempts key sectors such as oil and gas and petrochemicals.

Yet, as noted above, the need for foreign investment to finance Mexican growth will accelerate the pace of liberalization and thus lead to further harmonization of Mexican policies with those of its northern neighbors. We can thus expect lax enforcement and ultimate removal of performance requirements, and a smaller number of exempted sectors.

The real problem area—as in the US-Canada context as well—is the energy sector. Movement toward a unified North American market would have to allay strong sovereignty concerns in both Canada and Mexico. However, increasing US dependence on energy imports means that a NAFTA must include some energy supply access guarantees, akin to those contained in the US-Canada FTA. Any agreement in this area will have to overcome strong political opposition in Canada and Mexico; a possible solution may lie in the establishment of private trilateral energy consortia to engage in infrastructure investment in the North American market— perhaps initially limited to specific sectors such as natural gas in Canada and petroleum refining in Mexico.

Services

Liberalization of services trade between the United States, Mexico, and Canada is likely to be guided by the framework code of rights and obligations developed in the Uruguay Round (and based substantially on the US-Canada provisions). Such an accord probably will be designed to liberalize trade through an evolutionary process, sector by sector, starting from the baseline of existing policies.

While the GATT code will provide a good foundation for North American services trade, there will be substantial pressure for the three countries to go farther in financial services and in telecommunications, as the United States and Canada did in their FTA. Such a step would require both privatization and liberalization in these sectors in Mexico. The privatization of Telmex is a promising sign, as is Mexico's decision to denationalize its banking sector—which improves prospects for a financial services pact.

Labor services also will have to be addressed, though the large disparity in national wage levels will undoubtedly raise serious concerns from industries and workers likely to face increased competition—for example, sanitation employees or the construction industry. The US-Canada pact dealt only with trade in certain white-collar labor services. While a NAFTA could expand on those provisions, an attempt to cover a wide variety of labor services could prove fatal to the NAFTA process.

Consequences for the World Trading System

In sum, the task of building a more integrated North American economic community is worthwhile, but will not be easy. The best approach would be to make haste slowly, and follow the low road to regional integration.

Rather than conduct parallel talks bilaterally and in the GATT, the NAFTA process should be delayed until the Uruguay Round is completed. The United States, Canada, and Mexico could then build on the results of the GATT talks to further open the North American market.

As a first step, a group of independent experts from the three countries should be commissioned to analyze existing trade barriers in goods and services sectors, much like the McDonald Commission report in Canada in 1985 prior to the start of the US-Canada talks. The results of this analysis could help allay concerns in Canada that a US-Mexico bilateral or a broader free trade agreement would undercut benefits derived from the US-Canada FTA; it could also address concerns in other developing countries in the hemisphere that such agreements could result in a substantial erosion of their export trade to North America.

This latter point underscores the need for all three countries to be sensitive to the implications of a prospective NAFTA on their trade with third countries, and on their participation in the multilateral trading system. In this instance, political sensitivity dovetails with commercial practicality and geopolitical reality. A NAFTA should not lead to a discriminatory regional bloc in the sense of erecting new barriers against outsiders, because the United States (and to a lesser extent Canada) needs to pursue export-led growth and expand its trade with third countries in order to correct its external balance in the 1990s. More importantly, as architects of the postwar international economic system founded on multilateralism, both the United States and Canada have a strong ideological commitment not to prompt a race to regionalism.

References

Financial Times. (1989). October 18. 7.
————. (1990). March 19. 6.
Gurria, Jose Angel.(1990). "Mexico is on the move again." *Wall Street Journal.* March 9. A13.
Hufbauer, Gary. (1990). *Europe 1992: An American Perspective.* The Brookings Institution.
International Monetary Fund. (1990). *International Financial Statistics.* February.
International Trade Reporter. (1990). February 21. 256-257.
Johns, Richard. (1990a). "Mexico to open up in computer and drugs sector." *Financial Times.* February 9. 9.
Johns, Richard. (1990b). "Mexico defends plan to privatize stell plants." *Financial Times.* March 9. 6.
Mexican Ministry of Industry and Trade; Staff of Economic Advisor. (1990). *Tariff Elimination Between the United States and Canada: Effects on Mexico's Trade Flows.* Unpublished Report. Mexico City. Abstract.
Rogozinski, J., Ministry of Commerce and Industrial Development, Mexico. (1990) Speech on "Privatization in Mexico." Center for Strategic and International Studies. March 2.
Salinas de Gortari, Carlos. (1990). Speech before the contracting parties to the GATT. February 1.
Salinas de Gortari, Carlos. (1990). *Financial Times.* January 30. 6.
Trigueros, Ignacio. (1989). "A free trade agreement between Mexico and the United States?" in Jeffrey J. Schott, editor, *Free Trade Areas and US Trade Policy.* Institute for International Economics.
Washington Post. (1990). February 25. H6.
Womack, James P. (1989). "The Mexican motor industry: strategies for the 1990s." Paper prepared for the Mexico-US Business Council. May. 12.

6

Assessing the Prospects for North American Economic Integration

Charles F. Bonser

The movement of the US, Canada, and Mexico toward the eventual establishment of a North American Economic Community has begun. How far it goes, and at what speed, will depend on a number of variables. Most have been mentioned or alluded to in the four papers presented earlier in this volume, and were elaborated in the discussions held at the Wingspread Colloquium. In strategic planning terms, these determining variables can be evaluated in the context of an external "environmental scan" of the current world economic scene, and in an "internal scan" of those political and economic factors that are particular to the three nations involved. Let's first take a look at a scan of the external factors.

An Environmental Scan

The world trading system finds itself in 1990 in one of those pivotal periods that occur from time to time when choices are being made that could set the direction of history for many years into the future. Since the end of WWII, though we have experienced fits and starts, the nations of the world have been generally moving in the direction of expanding the opportunities for world trade. But there are several sets of discussions and negotiations now underway that some believe could change this pattern of increasing liberalization of the international trading system. The most serious of these are the negotiations in the Uruguay Round of the General Agreement on Trade and Tariffs (GATT); and the discussions going on in Europe, Asia-Pacific, and in North America about the establishment of regional trading systems—or as some refer to them—trade blocs.

The GATT Talks

The current round of GATT talks began in Uruguay in 1986, and are scheduled to conclude in December 1990. After 45 years, and seven rounds of negotiations and improvements, many believe the GATT is in trouble. Congressman Lee Hamilton (D.Ind.), Chairman of the Joint Economic Committee of Congress, in a July 1990 report to his district, commented, "the world market is in danger of being choked by a growing accumulation of restrictive measures. Industries demand protection; trading rules are increasingly being ignored and evaded; mechanisms to resolve disputes are unsatisfactory; bilateral trade agreements are proliferating. If the trends toward trade restriction continue, then sustained economic growth will be threatened."

In a recent speech before the National Press Club, US Trade Representative Carla Hills, said: "There is no question about it: This round of GATT talks is a bold and ambitious undertaking. It is the last, best chance this century to create the trading rules we need for the next century."

Yet, there are currently over 100 member nations of the GATT, and world trade shows no sign of slowing down. Since its establishment in the 1940s, the GATT has been very successful in being able to lower tariffs, and in providing an improved legal framework for conducting world trade. Other aspects of international business have lagged behind this progress. There has been a growth of non-tariff barriers, an increase in dumping, and little progress in opening the agricultural trading environment. Neither has there been much progress on easing the flow of business and professional services between nations.

The goals of US policy for the current Uruguay Round of negotiations is centered on reducing agricultural subsidies and other non-tariff barriers (such as import quotas and protectionist subsidies) to the free trade of agricultural products; to strengthen anti-dumping rules; to eliminate pirating and protect intellectual property (patents, copyrights, trademarks); to expand market access provide rules for "fair play" for trade in services (financial, telecommunication, engineering, professional services, etc.); and to ease investment rules to improve the international flow of capital. Market disruption and dispute settlement mechanisms are also targeted for improvement.

At a meeting of the leaders of the group of seven major industrial powers in Houston in July 1990, President Bush pressed the European Community nations present on the question of reducing agricultural subsidies and generally opening internal markets. The meeting saw an agreement among the chief executives to work toward that goal, but follow-up meetings among trade ministers have so far made little progress. In fact, if anything, the discussions have affirmed the difficulty the negotiators will face in trying to reach agreement. Agricultural production in Europe is still today heavily controlled by individual farmers, and 75% of EC agricultural production is based on some form of administrative pricing. The political difficulty of doing away with farm subsidies is obvious.

As noted by Congressman Hamilton, the upshot of this current situation is increasing concern that the current GATT talks will conclude without making significant progress. If that happens, one of the certain outcomes will be an acceleration in the interest in Asia, North America, and other parts of the world in the formation of regional trading blocs for both protection and economic purposes.

Regional Trading Blocs

In his commentary on the Lawrence Klein paper, Michael Musa reminded us that US opposition to trading blocs goes back at least as far as the Revolutionary War, when we were fighting a very important trading bloc known as the British Empire. In his words: "If you read the Declaration of Independence, after you get beyond the pursuit of happiness, what you find is a long list of unfair burdens on US commerce which the British Empire had imposed on the Colonials." This policy of opposition to trading blocs, and our promotion of free trade, has continued throughout our history, with occasional protectionist lapses such as Smoot-Hawley in the 1930s.

The Wingspread group reached no conclusion about the desirability, one way or another, of the recent trend toward the establishment of regional trading agreements. However, most concurred that the world would be better off in a multilateral trading system, and there was some concern expressed that the development of trade blocs would inhibit the expansion of GATT and its ultimate goal of opening world trade. Some believed, however, that regional trading organizations were inevitable, could be helpful in many ways, and that they did not necessarily have to be protectionist. As one observer put it, "trade blocs mean the reduction of barriers *behind* the borders but do not necessarily mean barriers *at* the borders." In fact, there is the view that blocs have the potential of functioning as laboratories. They can practice relationships and trading patterns on a smaller scale that are the eventual goal for the broader world trading system.

The major outside impetus for the current wave of discussions about the establishment of regional trading organizations in North America and in Asia-Pacific is the movement of the European Community toward a single market by 1993. Given the protectionist history of many of the European countries, some policymakers in Canada, Mexico, the United States, and in the Asia-Pacific region believe they may need to counter what appears to be the organization of a European trading bloc with regional trading systems of their own.

Peter Ludlow's paper makes a convincing case that the European Community is consciously developing into a trading bloc. If fact, he states that it already exists. In his words, "EC and EFTA (Austria, Finland, Iceland, Norway, Sweden, and Switzerland) are really the bloc . . . but we have remained open to the rest of the world." His argument is that the multilateral trading system cannot realistically function with the type of majority voting system needed to enact and enforce trading rules. Therefore, regional trading blocs—which are much more manageable—are needed to advance world trade.

The exact form that the EC-EFTA relationship will take is still very much open to discussion, and negotiations are now underway to design a common "European Economic Space." At the moment the majority view in the EC seems to be that the Community needs to focus on "deepening," rather than "broadening." In other words, they need to complete their movement toward a single market, and settle such issues as an agreement on monetary and economic union before they consider adding new members to the "club." The involvement of EFTA in EC policy would therefore be in "decision shaping," rather than "decision making."

Whether or not this relationship will actually hold remains to be seen. Clearly some of the EC leadership thinks of the Community as permanently maintaining its membership at its present level. This is a much easier route to "nation building" than would prevail if the EC were to bring in new members from either EFTA or Eastern Europe. However, EFTA, which now does 60% of its trade with the EC, may not realistically be willing or able to remain outside the Community with its only input on trade policy being "shaping" rather than "making." Furthermore, it may be politically difficult for the EC to keep them out. The Treaty of Rome that established the Community indicated that any democratic European Country with a market economy should be eligible to join. If some or all of EFTA joins the EC, which would be more likely after 1992 than before, Hungary, Czechoslovakia, and Poland are the next candidates.

Whatever form results from the evolution of the "New Europe," a *de facto* trading bloc will be the result. This does not necessarily mean that Europe will be more protectionist, or that the world will face a more restrictive trading environment. Rather, the arguments that the Europeans will need open markets themselves—both for internal and external purposes—suggests that they will trend toward the easing of trade restrictions and impediments as they get their own internal house in order. Abel Matutes, EC Commissioner from Spain, recently commented on this issue, arguing that the EC market will promote faster economic growth that will increase, not diminish the EC's commitment to open trade and generate higher demand for imports. "The EC will come out reinforced as the number one trading partner in the world, and therefore with a strongly reinforced interest in maintaining and developing a multilateral trading system."

One of the important reactions to these developments in Europe has been the activity generated in the Asia-Pacific region of the world. There have been discussions among the ASEAN countries (Brunei, Indonesia, Malaysia, The Philippines, Singapore, and Thailand) as well as the twelve-member, more broadly based Asia-Pacific Economic Cooperation organization (APEC), which includes Japan, the US, Canada, Australia, and New Zealand, about the dangers of a breakdown in the GATT talks. They expressed concern about the 1992 goals of the EC, and blamed the Community and their system of export subsidies for agricultural trade barriers for the GATT difficulties. As noted in the Introduction to this book, Australia will be hosting another meeting this year to discuss an Asia-Pacific regional economic cooperation organization.

Responding to APEC for the EC, Commissioner Matutes stated, "The EC will take a negative view . . . if the current initiative turns into a body for coordinating trade policies of players enjoying a preponderant part in world trade . . . The EC would oppose an Asia-Pacific group that sought to `pre-cook' the outcome of multilateral trade talks like GATT." Matutes noted that, if the US and Canada are included, "roughly 50 per cent of EC trade is with this region. That raises the prospect of 50 per cent of our trade being discussed in our absence and outside the framework of GATT."

Of course, the mirror image of that situation is what concerns those in the non-European parts of the world. It therefore seems inevitable that one result of the new European architecture, whatever form it takes, will be the development of trading organizations in other parts of the world. These will be formed in some cases strictly on their own merits, and in others primarily for negotiation purposes, and to act as countervailing forces to the increased power of the Europeans. The weight of argument is therefore in favor of the Lawrence Klein view that, while we are heading toward an expansion of global trade in the years ahead, a component of this trading system will be "trading zones held together by bilateral agreements or by a strong institutional framework, as in the case of the European Community."

One of the main worries about the movement toward trading blocs is the fate of those nations that will fall between the cracks. How will Latin America, Africa, and the other southern hemisphere nations fare in a trading environment dominated by regional trading organizations primarily made up of the industrialized nations?

These fears are understandable, but there are good arguments that the LDCs would also benefit from an expanding world trading system, assuming the blocs work to liberalize trade patterns. In other words, as George Wilson stated, "a rising sea floats all ships." It has also been suggested that, in the case of Latin America, the United States is particularly interested in helping the nations of that region develop their economies so as to enhance political stability, to offer them alternatives to the income from the north/south drug trade, and as a side benefit, to reduce the flow of migrants from the South. Discussions are scheduled for late this year on a new US relationship with the "Southern Cone."

The Europeans will be equally interested in seeing that the less-developed regions more relevant to that continent are not left out of an expanded world trading system. As the *Economist* recently pointed out (8/5/90), "Rich Europe is about to face an invasion from its poorer neighbors"—both from the south and from the east. The population of the three Maghreb countries— Algeria, Morocco, and Tunisia—"may double to 120 million or more over the next thirty to forty years. For many of these huddled millions, prosperity will seem just a boat trip away." Already the opening of East Europe has led to an influx of immigrants from those countries.

While one can argue that both Europe and the US need the new young blood from these less-well-off regions to shore up their own sagging labor markets, politically it will be difficult to absorb the numbers that could arrive if the LDCs do not share in the economic prosperity that will accompany an expansion of world trade. Therefore, while the impact of regional trading blocs on the Lesser Developed Countries is a legitimate concern, both market opportunities and practical politics suggest that the LDCs will not be forgotten or ignored.

An Internal Scan of North American Economic Integration Issues

The upshot of the "environmental scan" above is persuasive to this author that, while blocs may be a second-best solution, external factors in the world trading system are propelling the nations of the world toward a system based on regional trading agreements. Furthermore, while in the best of all possible worlds one would much prefer an open multilateral trading system, a trading bloc pattern of free trade agreements does not necessarily mean that we must retreat to a protectionist world with walls around the trading systems. As we noted earlier, Free Trade Areas are about breaking down internal barriers, not necessarily erecting barriers to the outside world.

Given this situation, what can we expect from—or suggest to—those who would be responsible for considering the establishment of a North American Economic Community?

For the moment, let's put aside the question of the US-Canada Free Trade Agreement (in spite of the complications recently created by the Quebec problem), and consider that FTA a "done deal." The questions then focus on the US-Mexican FTA possibility, and later, how and if such a trade agreement would be extended to include Canada.

The Economics and Politics of a Mexico-US Free Trade Agreement

Both Baker and Miller and Hufbauer and Schott deal with the politics and the economics of a trade agreement between the United States and Mexico. They also look to the future, and predict some form of legal overlay that would result in easing the flow of trade between the three countries. Hufbauer and Schott, particularly, argue for an approach they describe as a "low road to a low goal." In this case the "low goal" is a North American Free Trade Area (NAFTA), that would be reached 'step by step' over a long period of time." While the Baker and Miller paper is less specific about the details of such an agreement, they seem to support that general approach when they argue that there is a "need for a realistic period of transition to allow Mexico to adjust."

The Wingspread Colloquium served to elaborate and evaluate the political and economic arguments presented by the Miller/Baker and Hufbauer/Schott papers bearing on the Mexican-US FTA possibility. The economics of such an agreement are positive at present, but not compelling. Today Mexico exports about $27 billion per year to the US, and the US exports to Mexico approximately $25 billion. But the trade flows are increasing rapidly. Mexican exports to the US grew 20% in 1989 alone.

Much of the recent momentum in the growth of trade between Mexico and the US has resulted from the better economic position the Mexicans have been able to develop for themselves through the reforms of the 1980s. Baker and Miller covered this topic extensively in their paper. The fact that the Mexican government intervention in the economy has quickly retreated from a point where they controlled operations totaling 32% of GNP, to today's total intervention of about 18% of GNP, is really a remarkable achievement. This program of privatization is still underway.

In addition, the *maquiladora* Border Industrialization Program, that allows 100% foreign control of plant operations in Mexico under certain specifications, has also had a positive impact on Mexican export capability. The program permits duty free import of materials and equipment, provided that 80% of the output of the importing manufacturer would be exported from Mexico. On the US side of the border, low import duties are granted to products made by US manufacturers and assembled abroad.

Employment in the *maquiladora* zone has grown from about 110,000 in 1980, to almost 400,000 in 1989. According to Lawrence Klein, the *maquiladora* program now contributes about 5% to Mexico's GNP. He thinks this is "only a fraction of what could be achieved with a Mexican-US FTA and expanded world trade."

The program has also had sizable impact on those US cities and states bordering Mexico. The *National Journal* (7/29/89) reported that the Maquila payroll on Tijuana alone generates up to $93 million annually for the California economy. Since 1980, new construction for office buildings and warehouses in San Diego to service these industries has been estimated to have added significantly to San Diego's population, which grew from 1.9 million to 2.3 million.

One of the problems the *Maquiladora* Program has faced is the opposition of some of the US Labor Unions, who believe that the program is responsible for exporting jobs to Mexico that might otherwise go to US workers. Industries that are particularly sensitive, as Baker and Miller point out, are automobiles, textiles, and shoes, as well as other low-wage industries. There is also a concern that Japanese electronics firms, and other foreign manufacturing industries locating in the *maquiladora* zone, are somehow circumventing US law. In a way, this situation is a small sample of the opposition that could be generated against a possible US-Mexico Free Trade Agreement, and therefore warrants a closer look.

There is not much hard evidence available to support arguments one way or another that the *Maquiladora* Program in fact threatens US jobs. The econometrics of such an analysis are difficult, and so far not much research has been done on the topic. One study, conducted by William C. Gruben, was reported early in 1990 by the Federal Reserve Bank of Dallas in their monthly review (*Economic Review*, Jan.,1990). Gruben looked at the relationship between job growth, and wages in the *maquiladora* zone and those in the US, and an average of four of the PACNIC country wages (Hong Kong, Korea, Singapore, and Taiwan). He concluded: "*Maquiladora* job growth is sensitive to differentials between Mexican and US wages, but it is about equally sensitive to differences between Mexican and PACNIC wages." In other words, Mexican workers compete with workers in Asia, just as they do with workers in the US . . . . . "If all of the *maquiladoras* were shut down tomorrow, many *maquiladora* jobs would not return to the United States. Instead they would go to Taiwan, Hong Kong, Singapore, or Korea."

For those who are concerned that a US-Mexican FTA would drive down US wages, it might be worthwhile noting here that one of the Wingspread participants, Alfred Tovias, of the World Bank, reported that his own research suggests that most of the wage changes that would follow US-Mexican economic integration, would be on the Mexican side of the border, not in the United States. Another argument that could help ease US Labor concern is that with the current winding down of the American defense industry following the conclusion of the Cold War, there will be a substantial negative economic impact on the border states of the United States. Lawrence

Klein thinks an FTA with Mexico would help the economies of those affected states.

There are more traditional economic arguments that support the concept of Mexican-US integration. Several, such as the beneficial effects of competition on economic efficiency, were discussed by Baker/Miller and Hufbauer/Schott. There is also the view that recent economic reforms in Mexico have carried the expansion there about as far as possible, and the stability and impetus that a FTA would provide is necessary to attract new investment, bring back old Mexican money, and keep the economy moving ahead. An export led expansion would help Mexico solve its external debt and monetary stability problems.

On the positive side of the American end of the equation, one of the participants at the Colloquium pointed out that while the US has the technology and manufacturing know how, the American labor force is growing very slowly, if at all, and will need labor availability in the future. On the other hand, "Mexico will have more labor force entrants than the US next year, and this growing labor force is well-trained, competent, and capable of producing competitive goods at a low price. For the US, Mexico also offers a big and growing 'undernourished' market" that is short of most of the goods common to the average American family. In other words, the fit is good, at least for the long run.

Hufbauer and Schott also offer a few negative economic factors bearing on the issue. They argue that, if the US and Canada joined a NAFTA, the economic benefits would be marginal, at least in the short run. "Cold arithmetic suggests that the addition of Mexico to the US-Canada Free Trade Area would exert little impact on American or Canadian GNP or exports, since Mexico is small relative to its partners." They also suggest that in the long run, "The potential disruption to both the United States and Canada of an 80 million strong low-wage country working its way up the product chain are enormous . . . Canada, like the US, would gain from reciprocal exports of more sophisticated products. But an FTA would certainly accelerate the restructuring of both countries out of industries that have enjoyed protection from low-wage developing countries."

Primarily a Political Question?

Although a good case can be made for the positive economic effects on both sides of the border, it seems safe to say that the economics of a NAFTA, in and of itself, are probably not enough to move the three countries to a formal "legal overlay" agreement. If the agreement is going to come about, the internal politics of it are going to have to be very positive. On this aspect of the issue, opinions can vary widely.

One view expressed forcefully at the Colloquium was that it would be a political mistake for the US and Mexico to formalize their economic relations with "a piece of paper." Many of the economic relationships are already in process. Mexico has now shifted to a more export-oriented economy, and the US, unless it closes its doors, will be Mexico's major trading partner. Therefore, "much of the benefit that would be derived from a formal FTA is going to flow as the natural consequence of decisions that have already been made." A FTA would be a "hard political sell in Mexico," and in the US, Congressional opposition is likely to be greater than to the US-Canada FTA because of the stronger reaction of the US Labor movement. "Instead of trying to formalize the relationship, we should let it evolve gradually, and help Mexico participate in the Multilateral trading system." The down side of this approach, however, is that Mexico may have difficulty attracting the investment it needs without the stability that an institutional framework like an FTA would offer.

Several other negative political factors bearing on the possibility of a US-Mexican FTA were discussed at the Colloquium. They include the following:

- Some doubted the value of the "insurance" argument that a legal overlay (such as a FTA) would protect Mexico from protectionist measures by the US against Mexican manufacturers. The suggestion was that, from a Mexican perspective, this was an elitist view and would not be a politically popular argument. It is worth noting, however, that the insurance argument was critical in developing support in Canada for the US-Canadian FTA.

- A NAFTA would rely on US willingness to allow "decision shaping" on the part of the Mexicans as well as the Canadians. It was judged unlikely that the US would go very far in this direction, given what some regard as the marginal benefits it would receive.

- A NAFTA could eventually result in a very dramatic change in industry specialization between the countries. The politics of the perception of such a change will be very difficult in both Canada and the United States.

- If GATT succeeds in further liberalizing trade, interest in a NAFTA will fade.

- Concerted movement toward the establishment of a NAFTA, particularly before the completion of the Uruguay Round, will seriously undercut and erode the GATT system and our ability to strengthen multilateral trade. Those within the US Congress and the Administration committed to multilateralism will see NAFTA as a threat to that goal.

- A US-Canada-Mexico agreement would cause political difficulties with Latin American and Caribbean nations, who would feel left out of the tri-lateral process, and injured by a lack of progress in expanding multilateral trade.

- For the Canadians, the idea of a NAFTA holds little economic appeal. They have very little trade with Mexico (although some Canadian firms have recently expressed interest in the *Maquiladora* Program), and the possible loss of jobs that could result from a NAFTA would yield tough politics in the Canadian Parliament.

There are also several points made on the positive side of the internal political question. Some of the stronger of these are:

- Much of the attention of the US and the Europeans has recently been focused on changes underway in Eastern Europe, and how those economies can be strengthened. Yet, while "Mexico is bigger, more important to the US, and more dynamic than anywhere in Eastern Europe, it receives no direct aid from America." It is in the US interest to have a stable, prosperous neighbor on its southern border, and a Mexican-US FTA would advance that goal.

- In a recent article in the *Wall Street Journal* by Matt Moffett (7/9/90), it was reported that Mexico's need for foreign exchange has grown more urgent. A reduction in tariffs, and a stable exchange rate "have ignited a surge in imports." The deficit in Mexico's current account (the broadest measure of trade) is expected to be about $5 billion this year. Moffett suggests that the Mexicans have bought time through their sales of privatized firms, which have yielded $8-10 billion. They recognize they need the FTA to sustain progress.

- A free trade agreement would "help get government off the backs of manufacturers," protect the investment climate, and help lock in economic reforms the Mexicans have already made. Unless Mexico can increase its business investment, is given assured access to US markets, and is encouraged to continue its economic reforms, the country will begin to stall in its economic recovery. This would very likely lead to quite negative political results for both the Mexican government and the United States.

- Baker and Miller conclude: "Mexico is overwhelmingly locked into the US economy, and there is no real alternative: this [a NAFTA] is Mexico's only realistic option for creating growth and stability at home. The climate of protectionism abroad and the rise of trading blocs makes it imperative that Mexico consolidate its position with the United States as soon as possible, and that the accommodation should be one that provides an overall and lasting context for the freeing of trade—and later, capital and labor."

• The economic development of Mexico that would follow the establishment of a NAFTA would yield positive economic—and therefore political—benefits for several of the US states now threatened by military base closings and defense cutbacks. It would also reduce the pressure they are under from legal and illegal immigration from the south.

• As is evidenced by progress in paying their external debt, the Mexican leadership increasingly seems to believe that "statesmanship and long-term goals," rather than short-term political expediency, are the way to achieve respect for the government and progress for the country.

    President Salinas, in a recent speech to Mexican Labor leaders, made it clear that they need to help the country "increase productivity, lower costs, and help win markets inside and outside Mexico."

• The recent Iraqi conflict should make it clear, if it was not already, that the US needs to reduce its dependency on Middle Eastern oil. Mexico is already a significant supplier of oil to the United States, and has sizable reserves (estimated to be more than 50 billion barrels). But it is presently prevented from producing more oil because of a lack of production capacity. A Free Trade Agreement with the US that included a willingness on the part of the Mexicans to increase production and to allow foreign investment in the oil industry, would be tough politics for the Mexicans, but it would be a great political asset in the selling of the FTA to the US Congress and the American people.

• Gary Hufbauer reminded us of a James Buchanan comment to the effect that politicians are "history seeking." The establishment of a NAFTA holds the prospect of putting President Bush, President Salinas, and Prime Minister Mulrooney in the history books in a way that would never be accomplished by an expansion of the GATT.

Special Canadian Issues

Most of the above discussion has focused on the US-Mexican situation. That is hopefully understandable, due to the fact that the United States and Canada already have a Free Trade Agreement. In addition, as alluded to above, Canada is a long way from Mexico, and presently has very little economic interaction with the Mexicans. In fact, in the group discussions at Wingspread, some went so far as to say that the only reason Canada would join a Free Trade Agreement with Mexico would be for "altruistic reasons." Given recent interest by Canadian firms in the *Maquiladora* Program, and the attention that interest has brought from Canadian Labor Unions, that statement might be a bit too strong. But the point remains that Mexico is not presently high on the priority list of the Canadians.

In spite of that predilection on the part of the Canadians, it seems likely that a US-Mexican FTA would include, or be eventually followed by, a tripartite agreement to include Canada. As one of our participants put it, "the prospect of three independent, separately negotiated agreements doesn't make much sense." That situation could lead to such problems as inconsistent rulings and dispute settlements between the agreements. It would be much better for all concerned to have a coordinated North American Free Trade Agreement.

The Canada-US FTA is, of course, still new, and a long way (1998) from being fully implemented. But the economic interdependence of the US and Canada continues unabated, and it seems doubtful if the agreement will be derailed, even by a new government. As one individual put it, "The motivation behind the FTA is a rejection of a long-standing policy that the only way to create a nation is to erect trade barriers. In the absence of the FTA, it would have been difficult to maintain the Confederation."

The recent inability of the Canadian government to satisfy the French Canadians' demand for a constitutionally guaranteed distinct French Society, raises questions about the effect a division of the country along English-speaking and French lines would have on the Free Trade Agreement. Although the Canadian constitutional crisis happened after the Wingspread Colloquium was held, the answer that might have been inferred from our conversations held there is: "not much effect at all." The Canadians did not enter into a Free Trade Agreement because of political reasons, or because of any great love for the United States. They entered it because it made sense economically. They needed the guaranteed access to the US market that the FTA provided, and they did not want to chance being isolated in a world that might be dividing up into trading blocs.

The natural lines of trade in Canada are north/south, not east/west. If, in the worst case scenario, the Canadian Federation should disintegrate, it would continue to be in the interests of each of the separate provinces to continue strong economic ties with the United States. In fact, one could argue that it would be even more necessary for them to do so than if they were one united country.

The Bottom Line

The issue is difficult, and the arguments for the establishment of a North American Free Trade Agreement among Canada, Mexico, and the United States are far from being overwhelmingly conclusive. Those of us involved in the Wingspread Colloquium took no vote, and did not try to reach a consensus on the matter. Each of us is left with the problem of weighing the evidence and the arguments, and coming to his or her own conclusion.

For this participant, the weight of evidence comes down on the side of proceeding with the development of an agreement. I believe it would be in the interests of all three countries, and would place our continent in a stronger negotiating position in a world which is most likely dividing up into competing regional trading blocs. While the United States might be able to operate by itself in such a milieu, neither Canada or Mexico would be in as strong a position. Their fears that they might fall between the cracks in a trading bloc world is a legitimate concern. Irrespective of the economics of that scenario, it is certainly not in the political interests of the United States to have either Canada or Mexico operating economically at less than their potential.

It is understandable that some are concerned that the addition of a North American economic alliance to the world's trading system would do damage to multilateralism, and our hopes for improving the lot of those countries less advantaged than the industrialized nations. But events do not necessarily need to proceed in that fashion. In fact, one could make the argument that trading blocs, and their ultimate dependence upon each other in a global economy, will increase the openness of world trade—not reduce it. As one of our collegues put it, "the EC has contributed more to openness of markets than would be expected from any of the nations separately." If the Europeans, or other regional trading blocs, understand that restrictive trade behavior will induce retalliation from very large regional markets, they will be less likely to behave in a protectionist manner.

The arguments cited above about the self-interest of the industrialized nations in seeing that the southern hemisphere countries share in world-wide economic development also support the belief that the LDCs will not be forgotten in a trading bloc world. Surely the costs of ignoring the LDCs would greatly exceed the costs of including them in an expanded, multilateral trading system.

North American Economic Alliance Design Issues

So far there has been little information coming out of the US or Mexican governments about any of the particulars they have in mind for the free trade discussions that will open in December 1990. Clearly the US experience in setting up the Canadian FTA will be of benefit in providing a possible model. President Salinas has reportedly established six principles for the Mexican end of the negotiations. These are:

- sovereignty is not negotiable;
- a primary focus must be on the welfare of the Mexican people;
- a high priority for the Mexicans is the promotion of basic- and medium-sized industries;
- there should be reciprocity in all agreements;
- the implementation of any FTA should be gradual and allow for an orderly transition.

It will be remembered that the Hufbauer/Schott paper identifies two possible design goals for a North American Economic Alliance—a North American Economic Communty (NAEC) (the "high goal"), and a North American Free Trade Area (NAFTA) (the "low goal"). The political and economic realities of the present situation in the three countries supports their conclusion that a NAFTA is the way to go at this time.

Jeffrey Schott's work spells out in detail five basic areas for initial closer North American economic integration. These would be a good place for the negotiations to begin. In summary, they are:

- *Quota Liberalization*: Progress has already been achieved with the Mexicans in the past year, particularly in textiles and apparel, and in steel. The steel quota will vanish in 1992. The main problem area will be agriculture. Reform of price and other subsidies that distort trade between the three countries will probably need to wait for multilateral solutions under the GATT.

- *Tariffs*: The Canadian FTA calls for the elimination of tariffs by 1999. The Mexicans have now lowered their tariffs to a weighted average of 6.2%. The US will have to move more in that direction. Schott thinks all tariffs betweem the three countries can be eliminated by the year 2000.

- *Automobiles*: Canada and the United States have reached agreements that should evenutally result in a "level playing field in automotive production." Automobiles and parts are the largest part of manufacturing trade between the US and Mexico. Mexico is still essentially closed to the import of assembled cars. The goal should be a "North American automotive pact free of production and trade distortions."

- *Investment*: Mexico has a huge need for new investment. The reforms of the past year have allowed substantial progress, but more will have to be done to attract the necessary foreign investment. The US will also have to provide Mexico with secured access to American markets. The major problem area will be investment in the energy industry. Schott suggests that a private "Trilateral Energy Consortium," to engage in infrastructure investment in the North American market, may be one useful way to accumulate the necessary capital and to overcome political opposition to foreign investment in the national energy industries.

- *Services*: Trade in services will be based on the framework agreement being developed in the Uruguay Round of the GATT talks. Mexico will be pressed to do more in telecommunications and in financial services. The Mexicans will be interested in gaining more access to the US markets for engineering and construction services. Progress in opening the flow of labor services will be "problematic." The US-Canadian FTA agreed on holding the status quo on labor services. At a minimum, this locks in reforms to date, and provides a guarentee against losing ground on this touchy political issue.

Finally, as has been suggested several times elswhere in this volume, North American economic integration needs to proceed carefully, and at a deliberate pace. While one might hope for something closer to the "high road" (two- to four-year) timing for several major issues, the Hufbauer-Schott concept of "sketching the goal" and filling the details later makes sense. The major problem with stretching the process over too long a period is that the favorable national and international "constellations" seem to be lining up now. The right actors are in place, and outside events conducive to an agreement are occurring. If we wait too long, we may miss an opportunity to open a new era of cooperation on the North American continent, and a chance to help our neighbor to the south continue to pull itself into the modern industrial world. That would be in everyone's interest.

About the Contributors

Randall Baker is a professor and director of international programs at Indiana University's School of Public and Environmental Affairs. He has held posts as Lecturer at the University of East Africa in Uganda and as Senior Lecturer and Dean at the University of Anglia in Norwich, England. He has been a consultant for the British government, the World Bank, the United Nations, and the European Community, and has published extensively on development planning, environmental management, and international aid.

Charles F. Bonser is the Director of the Institute for Development Strategies and a professor in the School of Public and Environmental Affairs and the School of Business at Indiana University. He has held posts as Dean of the School of Public and Environmental Affairs, Associate Dean of the School of Business, Director of the Indiana State Tax and Financing Policy Commission, Director of the Intergovernmental Personnel Program for the State of Indiana, and Special Assistant to the US Secretary of Health and Human Services. He has been consultant/advisor to the Brookings Institution as well as a number of government agencies. In addition, he has substantial international experience in both university and foreign governments. He is a fellow of the National Academy of Public Administration, and was President of the National Association of Schools of Public Affairs.

Gary C. Hufbauer is the Wallenburg Professor of International Finance at Georgetown University. Formerly, he was a Senior Fellow at the Institute for International Economics, Deputy Director of the Georgetown International Law Institute, and Deputy Assistant Secretary for International Trade and Investment Policy for the Department of the Treasury. He is the author of 13 books and more than 50 articles on international trade, taxation, and finance.

Lawrence R. Klein is the Benjamin Franklin Professor of Economics and Finance of the University of Pennsylvania and founder of Wharton Econometric Forecasting Associates. He is past president of the American Economic Association and the Econometric Society. He is a member of the

American Academy of Arts and Sciences and the National Academy of Sciences and has been an advisor to the US government and international organizations. He has published extensively in economics specializing in econometrics, and in 1980 he was awarded the Alfred Nobel Memorial Prize in economic sciences.

Peter W. Ludlow is the Director of the Centre for European Policy Studies in Brussels, Belgium. He has held posts as Research Fellow at the University of Birmingham, Lecturer in History at the University of London, and Professor of History at the European University Institute in Florence, Italy. He has numerous publications, newspaper articles and broadcast in international history and politics such as "The Making of the European Monetary System," "Beyond 1992: Europe and its Western Partners," and "The Future of the International Trading System."

Joseph Miller is a professor at Indiana University's School of Business. He received a J.D. from the University of Chicago in 1963 and his Ph.D. in economics from the University of Wisconsin in 1970. He has received grant awards from the Ameritech Foundation, the Rockefeller Foundation, IBM, the US Department of Commerce, the Fulbright Commission, and the Ford Foundation. His current research focuses on problems of international competition and environmental impacts.

Jeffrey J. Schott is a research fellow at the Institute for International Economics in Washington, D.C. and adjunct professor of international business diplomacy at Georgetown University. He was formerly a senior associate at the Carnegie Endowment for International Peace, and an official of the US Department of the Treasury in the areas of international trade and energy policy. He has published numerous books and articles on international trade and US trade policy.

Participants

Randall Baker
Professor
School of Public and
    Environmental Affairs
Room 241
Indiana University
Bloomington, IN 47405

Luis Cardenas
Comptroller General
State of Hidalgo
Crater N/535
Pedregal de San Angel 04500
Mexico City, D.F.
MEXICO

Robert Clark
Director
US Trade and Economic
    Policy Division
Department of External Affairs
125 Sussex Drive
Ottawa, Ontario K1A0G2
CANADA

Larry Davidson
School of Business
BS 444
Indiana University
Bloomington, IN 47405

Norman Furniss
Professor
West European Studies
BA 542
Indiana University
Bloomington, IN 47405

Michele Fratianni
Professor
School of Business
Indiana University
Bloomington, IN 47405

H. Scott Gordon
Professor Emeritus
Department of Economics
Indiana University
314 Arbutus Drive
Bloomington, IN 47401

Jeffrey Hart
Associate Professor
Department of Political Science
Indiana University
Bloomington, IN 47405

Edward Hornby
Public Affairs Officer
Canadian Consulate General
12th Floor
310 South Michigan Avenue
Chicago, IL 60604

Gary C. Hufbauer
Wallenberg Professor
International School of Business
Diplomacy
Georgetown University
Washington, DC 20057

Bruce Jaffee
School of Business
BS 3024
Indiana University
Bloomington, IN 47405

Lawrence R. Klein
Professor
Department of Economics
University of Pennsylvania
Philadelphia, Pennsylvania 19104

John Koten, President
Ameritech Foundation
30 S. Wacker Drive
38th Floor
Chicago, IL 60606

Peter W. Ludlow
Director
Centre for European Policy Studies
33 Rue Duclae
B-1000 Brussels
Belgium

Joseph Miller
Professor
School of Business
Indiana University
Bloomington, IN 47405

Ingrid A. Mohn
Mexican Desk Officer
Room 3028
United State Department of
    Commerce
Washington, DC 20236

Hunter Monroe
Economist
Joint Economic Committee
1537 Longworth
House Office Building
Washington, DC 20515

Michael Mussa
Professor of Economics
Graduate School of Business
University of Chicago
1101 East 58th Street
Chicago, IL 60637

Angel A. Rogerio
Assistant to the Trade Commissioner
Trade Commission of Mexico
225 North Michigan Avenue,
Suite 708
Chicago, IL 60601

Edward Sanders
President
International Planning and Analysis
    Center, Inc.
450 Fifth Street, N.W.
Washington, DC 20001

Jeffrey J. Schott
Research Fellow
Institute for International Economics
11 Dupont Circle, N.W.
Washington, DC 20036

Larry Schroeder
Visiting Professor
School of Public and Environmental
    Affairs
Room 230
Indiana University
Bloomington, IN 47405

Manuel Suarez-Mier
Minister for Economic Affairs
Embassy of Mexico
1911 Pennsylvania Avenue, N.W.
Washington, DC 20006

Hans Thorelli
E.W. Kelley Professor of Business
 Administration
School of Business
Indiana University
Bloomington, IN 47405

Alfred Tovias
Consultant at the International
 Trade Division
The World Bank
Room S 8044, IECIT
1818 H Street, N.W.
Washington, D.C. 20433

Michael J. Varga
Economist/Foreign Service Officer
United States Department of State
Room 3425
2201 C Street, N.W.
Washington, D.C. 20520

George W. Wilson
Professor
Business and Economics
Indiana University
Bloomington, IN 47405

Howard R. Wilson
Director General
Trade Policy Bureau
Department of External Affairs
125 Sussex Drive
Ottawa, Ontario K1A0G2
CANADA

The "Institute for Development Strategies" (IDS) was initially established by the Indiana University Trustees in 1984 as the "Regional Economic Development Institute." The Institute was created to further research, graduate-level education, and scholarly exchange in the area of economic development and public policy. The Institute reports to both the University's Research and Graduate Development Office, and to the School of Public and Environmental Affairs.